THE POET LUCAN

Studies in Rhetorical Epic

M.P.O. Morford

New Edition

PAPERBACKS

VXORI DILECTISSIMAE

Cover illustration: from the frontispiece to N. Rowe, *Lucan's Pharsalia*,
London: Jacob Tonson, 1718.

First published in 1967 by
Basil Blackwell, Oxford

This edition published, with permission, in 1996 by
Bristol Classical Press
an imprint of
Gerald Duckworth & Co. Ltd
The Old Piano Factory
48 Hoxton Square, London N1 6PB

A catalogue record for this book is available
from the British Library

ISBN 1- 85399-488-X

Printed in Great Britain by
The Cromwell Press Ltd, Melksham, Wiltshire

PREFACE TO THE SECOND EDITION

T HE seven chapters of *The Poet Lucan* were part of a dissertation on *Some Aspects of Lucan's Rhetoric* written under the supervision of Professor Eric Warmington at the University of London and completed in 1963. The author was at the time Head of Classics at Lancing College in Sussex with a full-time teaching load, and to this day he remains profoundly grateful for the generosity with which Professor Warmington understood the pressures of completing doctoral work within three years under such circumstances. In preparing the work for publication the author removed two chapters, respectively on the importance of Valerius Maximus and the *Exemplasammlungen* for Lucan's material, and on the serpents in Book 9. This was a mistake, as Werner Rutz pointed out both in this *Lustrum* review and in private correspondence, since none of the published work since 1963 dealing with these topics has advanced them beyond what is to be found in the dissertation. Part of the chapter on the serpents was used for an article on Book 9 which appeared in *Latomus* 26 (1967) 123-29. The title submitted with the manuscipt was 'Death in the Desert', which was accurate: it was changed by the editor to 'The Purpose of Lucan's Ninth Book', which was not.

Readers of Lucan in 1996 will find it hard to realize how little attention had been paid to him before the 1960s. The editing of the text had been definitively completed, it seemed, by Housman, whose contempt for German scholars in particular, and in general for all people less intelligent than he, scared off most students from significant work on the text. Fraenkel's review of Housman (*Gnomon* 2 [1926] 497-532) has been generally undervalued by English-speaking scholars (and the bibliography to the present book is an example), while the work on which it was based at the Kiel Classical Seminar remains unpublished and impossible to obtain. The dissertation of H.C. Gotoff (*The Text of Lucan in the Ninth Century*, Cambridge, Mass.: Harvard U.P., 1971) attempted to prove that Housman's reliance on six manuscripts was an over-simplification, but it did not successfully challenge Housman's basic principle – that it is impossible to construct a stemma (see G. Luck in *AJPh* 96 [1975] 411-12). While Gotoff showed the way to move beyond Housman, substantial progress was made by L. Håkanson in his article, 'Problems of Textual Criticism and Interpretation in Lucan's *De Bello Civili*', (*Proceedings of the Cambridge Philological Society* 25 [1979] 26-51, and by D.R. Shackleton-Bailey in a series of articles in the same journal in 1981, 1982, and 1987, in preparation for his Teubner text of Lucan, published at Stuttgart in

1988. This is now the definitive text of Lucan. Meanwhile Georg Luck's unpretentious and reliable edition, with notes and a German translation (*Lukan: Der Bürgerkrieg*, Darmstadt: Wissenschaftliche Buchgesellschaft, 1975) has not had the recognition that it deserves. Housman's edition, which is valuable also for editorial notes that amount almost to a commentary, was reissued in 1951 (Oxford: Blackwell).

There is still no satisfactory complete commentary on Lucan in any language. The commentary by C.E. Haskins (London: Bell, 1887) is valuable chiefly for the Introduction by W.E. Heitland, which is vitiated by his prejudice in favour of Virgil. There is some value in the notes to the Budé text of A. Bourgery and M. Ponchont (3rd ed., Paris, 1962) and in Luck's edition mentioned above, but the curious student will have to go back to the editions of C. Schrevelius, with Farnaby's notes (Amsterdam: Elzevir, 1669) and F. Oudendorp (Lieden: Luchtmans, 1728) for substantial commentaries that appreciate the special qualities of Lucan's poetic style. In the last few decades, however, individual books have been issued piecemeal. The Pitt Press edition of Book 1 by R.J. Getty (Cambridge, 1955) remains in print (Bristol Classical Press, 1992), as does its companion for Book 7 by O.A.W. Dilke (1960, [revising J.P. Postgate, 1913], reprinted Bristol Classical Press, 1978). The edition by P. Lejay (Paris, 1894) is not easily accessible to English-speaking scholars, nor are the excellent commentaries by D. Gagliardi on Books 1 (Naples, 1989) and 7 (Florence, 1975). In the textbook series issued by the Cambridge University Press Book 2 has been selected to represent Lucan, in the edition by E. Fantham (1992). Commentaries on Books 3 and 5 have been issued as scholarly monographs, respectively by V. Hunink (Amsterdam, 1992) and P. Barratt (Amsterdam, 1979). There is no full commentary on Books 4, 6, 9, 10, beyond G.B. Conte's 'Saggio di commento a Lucano *Pharsalia* VI, 118-260: L'Aristia di Sceva' (Pisa, 1974, reprinted in *La Guerra Civile di Lucano*, Urbino, 1988) and M.G. Schmidt's *Caesar und Cleopatra: philologischer und historische Kommentar zu Lucan 10. 1-171* (Frankfurt, 1986). For Book 8 there is R. Mayer's perceptive commentary and translation (Warminster: Aris and Phillips, 1981), and for Book 9 the brief notes of D. Kubiak for the Bryn Mawr Commentary (Bryn Mawr, 1985). The early deaths of L. Håkanson and W. Rutz have been especially lamentable for scholarship on Lucan, the former with his work on the text unfulfilled, and the latter leaving us to regret that he could not continue his series of critical articles and bibliographical surveys.

For the Scholia scholars must still rely on the editions by J. Endt (*Adnotationes super Lucanum*, Leipzig, 1990: reprinted, Stuttgart, 1969), and H. Usener (*Commenta Bernensia*, Leipzig, 1869: reprinted, Hildesheim,

1967), although G. Cavajoni is updating Endt (*Supplementum Adnotationum super Lucanum*, Milan, 1979 [Books 1-5] and 1984 [6-7]). Scholars have fared better with lexical aids, having now M. Wacht's *Concordantia in Lucanum* (Hildesheim: Olms, 1992), which supercedes the Concordance of R.J. Deferrari, M.W. Fanning and A.S. Sullivan (Washington, D.C.: Catholic University, 1940: reprinted Hildesheim: Olms, 1965) and the Index of G.W. Mooney (*Hermathena*, Supplement 1, Dublin 1927).

In literary criticism and translation, however, the last two decades have brought a large number of publications of widely varying quality and durability. Before these are considered it will be helpful to the reader to say something about the way in which the present book was written in the 1960s, for the contrast between the quantity and the range of published scholarship then and now is remarkable. The author was trained rigorously in the study of the texts of Classical authors by J.B. Poynton and T.F. Higham, the former (to the best of the author's recollection of four years of intensive study under him) never once allowing in his classes criticism that was not based on a precise reading of the text. When the author began to teach Ancient History at Tonbridge School in 1952 he read Lucan to enrich his understanding of the period of the Civil War and of the significance of the war for the century between the deaths of Julius Caesar and Lucan. The power of Lucan's poem was overwhelming and its style compelling. These first impressions have not weakened over more than forty years. It was essential to come to Lucan with a secure knowledge of Homer, Virgil and Ovid, and consequently to be able to gain a profound respect for Lucan's originality within the epic tradition that he inherited. When the author began his dissertation he studied the declamations of Seneca the Elder and, helped by the fine work of S.F. Bonner (*Roman Declamation*, Liverpool 1949), began to understand the way in which the Virgilian tradition had been modified in what Frederick Ahl has felicitously called 'The Necessary Revolution'. The title 'Aspects of Lucan's Rhetoric' was appropriate, and the two Senecas and Quintilian (read in their entirety) provided the essential material for understanding the transformation of post-Virgilian epic. By the time the dissertation was completed the author had become primarily interested in Lucan's poetic qualities, and the title of the book ('The Poet Lucan') was perhaps more an optimistic expression of intent and was rightly criticised by Werner Rutz in *Gnomon* 39 (1967) 791-94.

Criticism of Lucan before 1960 had been thin indeed. Some of the earlier articles and dissertations were collected and published by Rutz in his *Wege der Forschung* volume on Lucan (Darmstadt: Wissenschaftliche Buchgesellschaft, 1970). The best work had been written by German scholars: representative were the article by E. Fraenkel, 'Lucan als Mittler des antiken Pathos' (*Vorträge der Bibliothek Warburg*, 1924, 229-57) and the dissertation by H-P. Syndikus, *Lucans Gedicht vom Bürgerkrieg* (Munich, 1958), both of whom brought precise reading of the text to a sensitive appreciation of the historical, poetic and emotional qualities of the poem. Rutz himself advanced understanding of the poem through his study of its structure in his Kiel dissertaion (*Studien zur Kompositionskunst und zur epischen Technik Lucans*, 1950), and R. Pichon had written the fundamental work of *Quellenkritik* in *Les Sources de Lucain* (Paris: Hachette, 1912), still valuable despite its Livian bias, and a significant achievement of French scholarship on Lucan. Appreciation of Lucan had languished in the English-speaking world, where Virgil reigned supreme and Ovid's *Metamorphoses* were not taken seriously – as is evidenced by the fact that during the four years that the author studied at the University of Oxford not a single course or even a single lecture on Ovid was offered. In 1945 Berthe Marti published a seminal article on 'The Meaning of the Pharsalia' (*AJPh* 66 [1945] 352-76, in which she argued for a Stoic reading of the poem and for Pompey as its central figure. Marti was convincingly rebutted by Rutz (see *Lustrum* 9 [1964] 267 and 271-72): nevertheless, her article remains one of the most stimulating publications in English and has enjoyed a revival with the recent interest shown in Lucan's Stoicism (e.g., D.B. George, 'Lucan's Cato and Stoic Attitudes to the Republic',*Classical Antiquity* 10 [1991] 237-58). The brief bibliography to the present volume reflects the paucity of studies of Lucan published before 1960, as does a comparison of R. Helm's bibliographical survey in *Lustrum* 1 (1957) 163-228, with those of Rutz in the same journal 9 (1964) 244-340 and 10 (1965) 246-59; 26 (1984) 105-203 and 27 (1985) 149-66.

The author, responding to reviews and suggestions made in private correspondence, completed a full-length study of Lucan in 1976. At exactly that time Frederick Ahl's *Lucan an Introduction* (Ithaca: Cornell U.P.) appeared and made the author's book unnecessary. Although it had been accepted for publication he withdrew it, a decision he now deeply regrets. Ahl's book has been an important element in making Lucan more accessible to English-speaking students, despite its shortcomings (see the author's review in *Classical Journal* 73 [1978] 272-74). The book does not show much concern with the epic tradition, the hallmark of German scholarship on Lucan, and in particular it virtually ignores Ovid. This defective approach has marked other recent books in English, notably the best one to appear so far, W.R. Johnson's *Momentary Monsters* (reviewed by the author in *AJPh* 110 [1989] 371-75). Johnson is provocative and lively, zealous to fly in the face of traditional approaches to ancient epic. More than anyone he has compelled readers of Lucan to take him seriously as a poet on his own terms, and to consider why his poem so powerfully presents a world in process of political, moral and social disintegration. Johnson's successors in the English-speaking world do not seem to be as methodical as he in their reading of the text. While some recent work has been stimulating, it seems that much speculative interpretation will not have lasting value over the years. More traditional approaches are still proving their worth, for example the book by W.D. Lebek (*Lucans Pharsalia: Dichtungsstruktur und Zeitbezug,* Göttingen, 1976). D.C. Feeney (*The Gods in Epic,* Oxford U.P., 1991) has advanced the study of a long-standing problem for Lucan's readers, and articles by E. Fantham on 'Caesar and the Mutiny: Lucan's Reshaping of the Historical Tradition' (*Classical Philology* 80 [1985] 119-31) and C.M.C. Green on '*Stimulos dedit aemula virtus*: Lucan and Homer Reconsidered' (*Phoenix* 45 [1991] 230-54) have kept alive the tradition of engagement with the poet's text at a time when other fashions of criticism have been more alluring.

It is hard to avoid the conclusion that real understanding of Lucan's text has become more rare as less time and effort for mastering his difficult Latin are allowed in the training of classicists. The acumen with which Grotius, Burman, Bentley, Housman or Fraenkel approached the text was as much the product of intimate familiarity with the rhetorical brilliance of post-Virgilian epic poetry as it was of those scholar's intellectual gifts. A by-product of the decline in general and assured familiarity with silver Latin poetry is, very probably, the florescence of translations that has marked the last few years. There have been three English versions of high quality, published respectively in 1988 (P.F. Widdows, Bloomington: Indiana U.P.), 1992 (S. Braund, Oxford U.P.) and 1993 (J. Joyce, Ithaca: Cornell U.P.). It will be regrettable if they prove to be substitutes for the Latin text itself, valuable as they are as antidotes to the clever and subversive Penguin translation of Robert Graves.

The bibliographical surveys of Rutz mentioned above are basic tools for Lucan, and because of them the author does not see the need to provide a new bibliography for this reprinting. Rutz' final survey was published posthumously in H. Temporini and W. Haase, *Aufstieg und Niedergang der Römischen Welt* II. 33 (Berlin: de Gruyter, 1985), with additions by H. Tuitje. The reader can see there vividly how the study of Lucan has expanded in the four decades since the initial publication of the present volume. As the previous pages have shown, there is still significant basic work to be completed: the need for a full commentary is most pressing. Needed also is a sympathetic essay on the importance of Ovid for Lucan (the only book-length study to date is the unpublished dissertation by O.C. Phillips on *The Influence of Ovid on Lucan's Bellum Civile,* Chicago, 1962). The

nature of Lucan's poetic achievement would be better understood with a
full-length study of his metrical usage, which has been dealt with chiefly
in the brief monograph of A. Ollfors (*Studien zum Aufbau des Hexameters
Lucans*, Stockholm, 1967) and the unpublished dissertation of L.O. Scher,
The Structure of Lucan's Hexameter (Stanford, 1972).

The reprinting of *The Poet Lucan* is an opportunity for the author to
acknowledge his gratitude to the many students and colleagues who have
shared his pleasure in this brilliant, perverse and powerful poet. After
more than four decades his enthusiasm is undiminished and his respect
for the text of the poem has continued to deepen. May this book stimulate
others to travel the same road!

Charlottesville, Virginia
January, 1996

PREFACE TO THE FIRST EDITION

THESE studies are substantially a revision of a doctoral thesis pre-
sented in 1963 at the University of London under the title *Some Aspects
of Lucan's Rhetoric*: in some cases, particularly in chapter IV, more detailed
arguments and fuller references will be found in that volume. I must here
acknowledge my gratitude to my supervisor, Professor E. H. Warmington,
for his kindly criticism and constant encouragement, and to Dr. O. A. W.
Dilke, who gave me much help and made many fruitful suggestions. I am
also grateful to Professor Berthe Marti, who allowed me to take advantage
of her own unpublished research; and to the Craven Committee of the
University of Oxford, who made a grant toward the expenses of travelling
to see Professor Marti. And I must express my appreciation of the stimulus
provided by Mr. J. C. Dancy, who encouraged his colleagues at Lancing
College to make teaching and research go hand in hand. The librarians
and staffs of several libraries have helped me substantially by their
courteous attentions: in particular I am grateful to the Librarians of the
Institute of Classical Studies in London; of the University of London
Library in the Senate House; of Birkbeck College; and to staff of the
Classical Reading Room in the Bodleian Library at Oxford. Publication
of this book has been aided by a generous grant from Birkbeck College
in the University of London.

My greatest debt is acknowledged in the dedication.

M. P. O. M.
The Ohio State University,   September, 1965.
Columbus, Ohio, U.S.A.

CONTENTS

INTRODUCTION

LUCAN has seldom been considered on his merits; critics, ancient and modern, have for the most part denied him a dispassionate approach. From Petronius to Robert Graves he has been generally condemned for being tainted with the vices of declamation, to such an extent that his claim to be called a poet has often not even been considered. The assumption which underlies this prejudice is that a Roman epic poet should be judged by reference to Virgil; a poet who fails to conform to the Virgilian canons of taste and technique has failed as a poet. This is explicitly stated by Quintilian, of ancient authors, who prefaces his remarks on Roman epic poetry with *laudes Vergilii* (10. 1. 85-6) in which Virgil is established as the standard by which all others fail. A similar attitude is implicit throughout Heitland's essay, which may be taken as representative of modern criticism (although it was published eighty years ago). It is a remarkable fact that one of Rome's most powerful authors should have been unfailingly subjected to such inadequate critical techniques and denied the right to be considered with reference to the circumstances, tastes and traditions of his own time. How many modern poets would survive the test if their critics judged them principally on the basis of a comparison with Milton?

In these studies, then, an attempt will be made to lay the groundwork for a juster estimate of Lucan as a poet. Their starting-point will be Quintilian's judgement (10. 1. 90)—*Lucanus . . . magis oratoribus quam poetis imitandus*—in which the antithesis between poets and orators implies that he who is the one forfeits claim to be the other as well (that Quintilian himself realized that he was not being completely honest may be inferred from the apologetic *ut dicam quod sentio*). No one of course can deny the existence of rhetorical epic; few, however, would attempt to define the phrase. In these pages certain common rhetorical themes, prominent in Lucan, together with their development in Roman literature, are examined, and in this way, it is hoped, some light will be thrown upon the meaning of 'rhetorical epic'. The range of these studies is limited, for they are concerned only incidentally with the political aspects of Lucan's rhetoric, nor do they seek to analyse his use of *pathos*, which is so important a feature of his style.[1] They are, then, preliminary to a comprehensive study of Lucan, but they lay groundwork that is essential for an unprejudiced estimate of his work.

In the first chapter the elements of formal school rhetoric of the first century A.D. are set forth, so that the reader can have before him the rules of declamation in which Lucan was trained. To give an idea of how Lucan actually applied these rules, five declamatory passages are then analysed: in this way the fact of Lucan's rhetorical mastery is established. The chapter closes with the speech of the Egyptian courtier before Caesar; since in the poem this scene is immediately followed by the diatribe against Alexander the Great, the first rhetorical theme to be considered, in the second chapter, is Tyranny. It is well known, of course, that Lucan was concerned throughout his poem with the evils of Caesarism, and the denunciation of Alexander is the most outspoken passage related to this theme. Less obvious, however, has been the relevance of the denunciation to the development of the poem, and this is considered in the discussion and analysis which follow. Lucan's Alexander is shown not to have been introduced so much as a declamatory *locus* as to have been used· just at that point of the poem where a climax in the attacks on Caesar was required.

Another example of a declamatory theme being used in the *color* of the delineation of Caesar is the Storm (5. 504–677). Before this is analysed, however, a thorough consideration is given to the place of the storm in Roman literature and declamation, so that the relationship of Lucan's declamatory technique to his epic is once again demonstrated. Caesar's storm is not the only one in the work; in the fourth chapter, then, it and the three other major storms are considered, along with the large number of similes which are connected with meteorological phenomena. Thus it becomes apparent that the sea and storms particularly interested Lucan; that his observation of them was not merely drawn from school-books and that he often succeeded in integrating these subjects into the development of his epic—in other words, that his declamatory material was, in intention at any rate, subordinate to the design of his work.

Lucan was less successful with divination and magic, in particular necromancy, and the Erictho episode (6. 413–830) is perhaps the place in the work that his detractors may most justly point to. Yet

---

[1] See K. Seitz, 'Der Pathetische Erzählstil Lucans', *Hermes* 93 (1965), 204. Also E. Fraenkel, 'Lucan als Mittler des Antiken Pathos', *Vorträge der Bibliothek Warburg* 1924, 229: A. Thierfelder, 'Der Dichter Lucan', *Archiv f. Kulturgeschichte* 25 (1934), 14.

the discussion of this passage and of the other principal sections concerned with divination (1. 522–695; 5. 67–236) again reveals Lucan's minute knowledge of his subject and his purpose—admittedly not successfully realized—of integrating these passages into the structure of the poem. Other conclusions follow from this examination; for example, the brilliance of Lucan's description of witchcraft compared to that of Ovid, or his conscious effort to contrast his own sixth book with the sixth *Aeneid*.

The last rhetorical theme to be discussed is the Dream, a standard feature of Roman epic, as were Storms and the Occult. In chapter 6 the four visions of the poem are analysed and their place in the structure of the work considered; they will be found to be particularly important as devices for aiding rhetorical *color*, in this showing again how Lucan employed his declamatory skill in composing the poem.

These four subjects—the Tyrant Alexander, the Storm, the Occult, the Dream—are apparently unrelated, yet together they provide valuable material for an estimate of what is involved in rhetorical epic. The final chapter of the book, then, reconsiders Quintilian's comment in the light of the preceding discussion. The reality of Lucan's shortcomings as a poet is not denied and some attempt is made to see precisely what it is that his critics are attacking. Much of the criticism is disarmed if (as has been suggested above) consideration is given to the culture of the age in which Lucan lived: yet faults remain, and even the well-disposed may still be unwilling to grant Lucan a place on Parnassus. A full assessment of the claims of rhetoric and poetry is not attempted in this book; but it does conclude that much remains after the rhetoric has been stripped away— in particular a feeling for the tragedy of Man and many glimpses of a brilliant epic technique—that will justify us in referring to the poet Lucan.

Chapter I

THE ELEMENTS OF LUCAN'S RHETORICAL TECHNIQUE

A SURVEY of the basic elements of Lucan's rhetorical technique will necessarily be brief, for, as Quintilian remarked (9. 3, 11), there is a Figure for every form of solecism; there could be virtually no end to an exhaustive catalogue of Lucan's figures and tropes, nor could such a catalogue do justice to the richness of Lucan's genius.[1] Quintilian distinguished five basic divisions of the art of oratory (3. 3, 1: cf. 8. *Praef.* 6): these are *inventio, dispositio, elocutio, memoria, pronuntiatio.* The first three are particularly important and relevant to the present discussion; for oratory consists of Matter and Words, and the pupil must study *inventio* for the former, *elocutio* for the latter, *dispositio* for both. In all he must bring *ingenium, cura, exercitatio* to bear on his composition, for only thus can he find the elements for his oratory, which are *sententiae, verba, figurae, colores* (Quint., 7. 1. 40). In considering Lucan's style one must always give a prominent place to the plan of his themes (*divisio*), to the pointed comments and epigrams which illuminate them (*sententiae*) and, above all, to the tone of each passage, which presents the facts in a particular light (*color*).[2]

The duty of the orator, said Quintilian, is *docere, movere, delectare*; it is in the sphere of *elocutio* that he would expect to be most concerned with *delectatio*, that is, with giving pleasure to his audience while he seeks to persuade them, mixing, as Horace advised, *utile* with *dulce*. The study of *elocutio*, then, is of the greatest importance in the orator's training; its achievement is defined by Quintilian as 'omnia, quae mente conceperis, promere atque ad audientes deferre' (8., *Praef.* 15); if the orator has not mastered *elocutio*, adds Quintilian, the other weapons in his rhetorical armoury will be as useless as a sword in its sheath. In rhetorical precept, where the student's ambition is to persuade his audience—whether it be judge, jury or assembly—the five divisions of the art of oratory all have their importance. But in the studies of the declaimer, whose hope is as

---

[1] The method is employed by R. J. Getty, Introd. to his ed. of Book 1 (Cambridge 1955), sect. 5, pp. xliv–lxvi; and attacked (uncharitably) by C. J. Fordyce in his review of Getty, *C.R.* 54 (1940), 95–8.

[2] Quint. 8. 5 (*sententiae*); 7. 1 (*divisiones*); 4. 2, 88–100 (*colores*).

much to win applause as to persuade, *elocutio* will predominate; for
where the content of a speech cannot lead to decisions or action, its
style will be all-important. This is true equally of the poet; and
Lucan, trained in the schools of declamation, shows in his epic that
the study of *elocutio* was dominant in his rhetorical training. Thus
we shall find that, however completely he learned the precepts of
rhetoric, his practice was that of the declaimers: the task undertaken
in the present studies is to find out whether Lucan, as Quintilian
seems to imply, was merely a declaimer or whether he can still lay
claim to the title of poet as well. In this chapter we shall analyse
a number of rhetorical passages in Lucan, so as to illustrate his
mastery of the rules of rhetoric. Since *elocutio* is concerned with
words and their presentation, tropes and figures are prominent in
its technique, as will be apparent in the analyses. It will be as well,
however, to preface these with some introductory remarks about the
chief types of speech and the rules for the structure of a speech.

According to the most widely accepted view there were three
types of speech—demonstrative, deliberative and forensic. Quinti-
lian was particularly concerned with the third of these, but in a poet
or historian few examples of such speeches (*genus iudiciale*) will be
found—a possible example in Lucan is 9. 1014–1032, which is
analysed below. The fivefold division of a speech applied particu-
larly to this type; the sections were *Prooemium* (*exordium*), *narratio*,
probatio, *refutatio*, *peroratio* (*conclusio*) (Quint. 3. 9, 1). Since most (if
not all) of Lucan's speeches are of the other two types, it is not
usually possible to divide them into the five parts. Most of them
contain *exordium* and *peroratio*, and in the latter Lucan usually intro-
duces his most telling points and memorable *sententiae*. It is here
that he appeals most directly to the emotions—'hic, si usquam, totos
eloquentiae aperire fontes licet . . . tunc est commovendum theatrum
cum ventum est ad ipsum illud . . . *plodite*' (Quint. 6. 1. 51–2).

In deliberative speeches (the commonest type in Lucan) the
speaker usually states his theme in or immediately after the *exordium*
(this statement is called κατάστασις): he then passes straight to his
discussion of the theme (*tractatio*) before concluding, generally with
a telling *sententia* (*conclusio*). *Narratio* is generally dispensed with,
and sometimes there is not even an *exordium* (e.g. Luc., 8. 331). In
the *tractatio* the speaker considers the expedient and the honourable
(*utile, honestum*),[1] and these subjects involve various subdivisions,

---

[1] Quint. 3. 8, 1: cf. Cic., *De Inv.* 2. 156.

such as *fas, iustum, pium*; *facile, possibile*; *magnum, gloriosum*. Throughout such speeches the aim is often to arouse the emotions (Quint. 3. 8, 12), and in such cases the rules for arranging the parts of a speech are of secondary importance. In any case it is often difficult to analyse Lucan's speeches, for the transitions (from part to part) are made as smoothly as possible: perhaps this feature is due to the influence of Ovid, for Quintilian specifically cites Ovid as a perpetrator of the 'frigida et puerilis adfectatio' of passing from section to section by means of a *sententia* (4. 1, 77: *ut Ovidius lascivire in Metamorphosesin solet*). Certainly it is a notable feature of Lucan's style, whether it comes from the schools or from Ovid.

Narratio is 'rei factae . . . utilis ad persuadendum expositio' (Quint. 4. 2, 31): it should be *aperta atque dilucida*, its words neither *sordida* nor *exquisita* (4. 2, 36); it should be credible, true to nature (*ib.* 52) and should have μεγαλοπρέπεια and ἐνάργεια (*ib.* 61–3); its *color* should fit the facts (*ib.* 90). At the same time it should be adorned *omni gratia et venere* (*ib.* 116): appeals to the emotions should be allowed (*ib.* 111), but these should be short and not as powerful as those at the end of a speech (*non diu neque ut in epilogo*). Digressions are permitted, provided that they are short and appear to be forced upon the speaker by the power of his emotions (*ib.* 104). It is here that the gulf between the declaimer and the advocates begins to widen: as Quintilian recognizes, the former would be hard put to it to make the unadorned statement of facts (*narrationis gracilitas*) sustain their performances—*ne dilatis diutius dicendi voluptatibus oratio refrigescat* (4. 3, 2). And so, in the declaimers' schools, the digression came to be almost a separate part of the speech.[1] It could embrace 'laus hominum locorumque, descriptio regionum, expositio quarundam rerum gestarum vel etiam fabulosarum' (Quint. 4. 3, 12). Cognate to the digressions were *loci communes*, which could be inserted as desired, a device that was much abused (Quint. 2. 4, 22–32).

The importance of *narratio*, with its extensions to the digression and *loci communes*, in Lucan's style can hardly be exaggerated:[2]

---

[1] Quint. 4. 3, 2: *natum ab ostentatione declamatoria*. The t.t. was *egressus* or *egressio*, Gk. παρέκβασις. Quint. uses *excurrere* (4. 3. 1) and *excursio* (4. 2. 104). See. S. F. Bonner, *Roman Declamation* (Liverpool, 1949), 57–60.

[2] Representative examples (cf. Heitland's introd. to Haskins' ed., London 1887, lxxii–lxxvii) are the digressions on Gaul (1. 392–465), Thessaly (6. 333–412), the Nile (10. 194–331); for mythological digressions, the legend of Antaeus (4. 593–660); legends of Lake Tritonis and the Hesperides (9. 348–67). See L. Eckardt, *Exkurse und Ekphraseis bei Lucan* (Heidelberg, 1936). Typical *loci communes* at 9. 573–84 (cf. Sen., *Suas.* 4) and 10. 108–71 (cf. Petronius, *Bellum Civile* 1–60).

hardly any other feature marks the difference so clearly between the structure of Virgilian epic and the *Bellum Civile*, and it is a mistake to approach this aspect of the poem with a mind prejudiced towards condemnation. The digressions, descriptions, *loci communes*—all are part of the poem, whether or not they impede the flow of the story. They were an essential part of the declaimer's armoury, and the taste of Lucan's age expected and delighted in such passages.

We may now examine some passages representative of Lucan's rhetoric; the analyses will introduce further details about *elocutio* which will again emphasize the importance of its study in forming the style of declaimer and poet.

A. DEMONSTRATIVE

An important subdivision of this type of speech is Panegyric, 'directed to the praise of Gods and men', even of animals and inanimate objects (Quint. 3. 7, 10–18).[1] Two obituaries are here taken as examples.

1. Luc. 4. 799–824. *The panegyric on Curio.*

Curio has already appeared in the first book, where he accompanies the expelled tribunes to Ariminum and with a rousing speech (1. 273–291: its theme is 'tolle moras: semper nocuit differre paratis', 281) feeds the flames of Caesar's eagerness for civil war. In Book 4 he is the central character of the last part of the book (582–824), although Lucan appears to be as much interested in him as an example of a type as for his particular character and exploits.[2] In both books his part is ambivalent: he is *audax* (1. 269; 4. 583: cf. 4. 702) yet he is also *vox quondam populi libertatemque tueri ausus* (1. 270–1). There is courage and a certain heroic quality about his leadership in Africa, which is shown by his soliloquy (4. 702–710) and by the manner of his death—

> non tulit adflictis animam producere rebus
> aut sperare fugam, ceciditque in strage suorum
> inpiger ad letum et fortis virtute coacta
>
> (4. 796–8: cf. Caes., *B.C.* 2. 42).

Therefore the *color* of the panegyric is twofold: Curio was the corrupted turncoat who precipitated the Civil War (4. 819); yet he

---

[1] For its corollary, Denunciation, see Quint. 3. 7, 19–22: cf. Luc. 7. 847–72; 8. 823–72.

[2] The African episode is allotted 243 lines, of which 70 (591–660) are given up to the Antaeus digression and 25 to the panegyric, leaving less than 150 lines for the whole of Curio's adventure. Another example of perverted virtue—typified by Curio—is Scaeva (e.g. 6. 262).

was a Roman of rare gifts who did much for Rome so long as he acted constitutionally. And so he earns his meed of praise (4. 813). The scheme is as follows:

799–809. Curio's part in precipitating the Civil War. The first six lines apostrophise Curio, and from his particular instance the poet draws a general moral (805–9),[1] closing the passage with a *sententia* in which *libertas* is the dominating theme. The *color* is given especially by 803–4, which imply that the reward Curio hoped for by his actions was to see the disaster of *dira Pharsalia*.

809–813. By use of the figure ὑποτύπωσις (*sub oculis subiectio*)[2] the poet brings the dead Curio before our eyes. Such ἐνάργεια (vivid description: cf. Quint. 8. 3, 61–71) heightens the pathos and so prepares the hearer for the panegyric which follows.

814–824. The panegyric itself: 814–15 refer to the good side of Curio (*recta sequenti*); 816–824 to his corruption and its fatal results. Into this passage is worked a *locus* against luxury and wealth (816–820), money being the cause of Curio's change of side.[3] The final epigram (824) is prepared by three lines of historical allusion, where the list of Roman tyrants is invoked to show that Curio's crime is unique—for he alone had the power to withhold his country's liberty (cf. 808–9) from the rapacious hands of the tyrant.[4]

2. Luc. 9. 190–214. *Cato's panegyric on Pompey.*

The apostrophe on Curio is among the most eloquent and persuasive lines of the poem. Equally impressive are Cato's lines on Pompey, although the character of Pompey is less compelling than

---

[1] *Potentes* (806) recalls the description of Curio at 1. 271. In 1. 291 (end of Curio's speech) *potes* may well mean 'you have the power to . . .'

[2] See Quint. 9. 2, 40–1, and *ib.* 42–3 (for the abuse of *subiectio* by the declaimers): Petr., *Sat.* 1 for a parody.

[3] Cf. Virg., *Aen.* 6. 621–2: vendidit hic auro patriam dominumque potentem / inposuit; fixit leges pretio atque refixit. For luxury as the cause of the war, cf. Petr., *B.C.* 1–60, esp. 49–50.

[4] The three *potentes* are each given an epithet—Sulla *potens*, Mariusque *ferox* et Cinna *cruentus*: we infer that all three epithets apply to the 'Caesareae domus series'. The following tropes and figures may be noted in the passages (references are to Quintilian): *antonomasia* (8. 6. 29)—802 (gener atque socer); 803 (dira Pharsalia): *epithet* (8. 6, 40)—803 (dira); 816 (perdita); 817 (metuenda); 818 (dubiam); 822: *hypallage* (8. 6, 23)—800 (tribunicia plebeius signifer arce): *metaphor* (8. 6, 4) 800 (signifer arce); 809 (vindicta); 813 (praeconia); 818 (transverso torrente); 819 (momentum): *metonymy* (8. 6. 23)—799 rostra forumque *for* rem publicam); 801 (arma *for* bellum); 819 (mutatus Curio *for* mutatio Curionis): *synecdoche* (8. 6, 19)—806 (iugulo, part for whole, cf. 821): *adiectio* (9. 3, 28–49)—805–6 (has . . . ferre datis / luitis sic): *alliteration*—803; 810; 813; 814; 818; 819; 821: *allusion* (cf. Bonner, p. 62)—799–801; 822: *antithesis* (9. 3, 81)—808–9 (cura . . . vindicta); 824 (emere omnes . . . hic vendidit): *apostrophe* (9. 2, 38)—799–804; 805–6; 811–13: *question* (9. 2, 6)—799–802; 823–4: ὑποτύπωσις —809–10.

that of Curio. Both were equivocators; but whereas (according to Lucan) Curio was first wholly good and then wholly bad, Pompey's whole life was ambiguous. Lucan's task, then, in composing his panegyric requires subtlety: the resulting *tour de force* is achieved not by power (as in the case of Curio), but by a subdued tone. There is no exclamation or apostrophe used in the panegyric itself (i.e. down to 203): it is a sustained exercise in *diminutio*, as opposed to the commoner (and technically easier) *amplificatio* (Quint., 8. 4). The chief techniques used are antithesis (which exploits the ambiguity of Pompey's public life) and simplicity of diction, which is achieved by the use of short disconnected sentences, often terminated at the end of a line. There is no other passage where Lucan has attempted so successfully to conceal his art.

Lucan has made all this possible by his arrangement of the poem after Pompey's death; Cato's speech is the second obituary, and what Cato omits here has already been said.[1] Cato, then, can praise Pompey adequately without being inconsistent with his own *gravitas* and *modestia*. His words are few and austere, but they are the truth (9. 188–9): this brief and simple panegyric, says Lucan (215–17), was more eloquent than the showpieces of the public orators.

The opening lines contain the *color* of the speech:

> civis obit, inquit, multum maioribus impar
> nosse modum iuris, sed in hoc tamen utilis aevo,
> cui non ulla fuit iusti reverentia.

The simplicity of the first two words is deceptive: *civis* is emphatic —Pompey was a Roman to the end and died leading the cause of liberty. But (and here is the second element in the *color*) he was inferior to the old Roman patriots, yet good by the standards of his age. The rest of the panegyric (to 203) expands this double theme in a series of antitheses which show how, on the one hand, he was far below the old Romans in knowing 'the limits of the law' (191), yet, on the other, displayed that *iusti reverentia* which was lacking in his contemporaries. The antitheses are as follows:

potens	. . .	salva libertate (cf. 1. 271; 4. 806)
plebe parata servire sibi		solus privatus
rector senatus	. .	regnantis (*sc.* senatus)
quae dari voluit .	.	voluit sibi posse negari

[1] Principally at 8. 806–22 (survey of career); 8. 639–61 and 9. 55–108 (grief of Cornelia); 8. 759–75 (Cordus); 9. 126–45 and 148–64 (sons of Pompey). Cf. 1. 129–43; also the dream at 7. 7–44.

poposcit . . .	dari voluit
inmodicas possedit opes	plura retentis intulit
invasit ferrum . .	ponere norat
praetulit arma togae .	pacem armatus amavit
iuvit sumpta . .	iuvit dimissa potestas
clarum gentibus . .	multum nostrae quod proderat urbi.[1]

The panegyric ends (203), as it had begun, with reference to Pompey's patriotism and his services to Rome.

The rest of the speech, which considers the consequences of Pompey's death, is quite different in character; at times it is Lucan, not Cato, who speaks. The antitheses are more forced (e.g. *vera* / *ficta* in 204–6) and the figures are more extravagant:[2] Cato obtrudes his own personality in the closing lines (212–14). Not only have the subject and the technique changed; the *color* is different, the keynote now being *libertas*, contrasted with *regnum*. Pompey was favoured by Fortune in being compelled to die when he might have agreed to live under Caesar's tyranny (210–11): but for Cato no such compromise is thinkable, and for him a voluntary death is the only alternative to liberty. Thus the speech, which had begun with reference to Pompey's death, ends by looking forward to Cato's.

B. DELIBERATIVE

This is by far the commonest type of speech in poets and historians, and includes battlefield exhortations. Two examples are given here, the first of which shows the close relationship between this type of oratory and the Suasoria.[3] In composing deliberative speeches Lucan observes the rule that one must bear in mind the subject under discussion, the character of those who are deliberating and the character of the speaker (Quint. 3. 8, 15). Sometimes this has unfortunate results, as in the quasi-judicial speech at 9. 1014–1032, where the repellent character of the speaker is so faithfully maintained that the speech loses most of its persuasive force: in other cases, for example Cato's desert speech (analysed below), Lucan is more successful.

[1] The other figures and tropes used (with references to Quintilian) are: *adiectio* (9. 3, 30–4)—196 (with chiasmus); 199 (arma / armatus); 200: *alliteration*—190; 193–4; 199; 201: *emphasis* —190 (civis); 191 (hoc); 194 (privatus); 195 (regnantis); 200 (ducem): *hyperbaton* (8. 6, 62–7)—193–4 (*privatus* misplaced): *isocolon* (9. 3, 80)—197–8 (inmodicas . . . opes / plura . . . intulit); 199 (praetulit . . . togae / pacem . . . amavit): *metonymy*—199 (arma togae: cf. Cic., Fr. 16 (Traglia), . . *De. Off.* 1. 77 'cedant arma togae'): *paradox*—194–5; 196; 199; 200.

[2] *Allusion*—204: *apostrophe*—208–10: *hyperbole*—206–7; *paradox* (with *irony*—Quint. 9. 2, 44)—208–9; 214: *sententia*—211.

[3] See Heitland (Introd. to Haskins' ed.) lxx–lxxi for a list of deliberative speeches.

1. Luc. 4. 476–520. *The speech of Vulteius.*

Vulteius and his men are trapped at sea on their craft: their choice is either to surrender at dawn or to die by their own hands. Vulteius advises suicide.

Suicide was a favourite theme of the Stoics,[1] and some such Suasoria as 'an milites obsessi hostem deprecentur' must have been a common school subject. The sixth Suasoria of Seneca is 'Deliberat Cicero an Antonium deprecetur': Seneca says that few declaimers argued in favour of begging for mercy (Sen., *Suas.* 6. 12). In the *divisio* he notes that Latro said: 'turpe esse cuilibet Romano . . . vitam rogare; . . . vilis illi vita futura est et morte gravior detrecta libertate' (*ib.* 8). Cestius (*ib.* 10) made the following *divisio*: 'mori tibi utile est, honestum est, necesse est, ut liber et illibatae dignitatis consummes vitam.' These two quotations cover much of Vulteius' argument: the following is an analysis:

Exordium. 476–7 (including statement of theme).

You have freedom for one night only; what will you choose when day breaks?

Tractatio. 478–514.

A. *Ab auditoribus.*

a. (*honestum,* including *utile* and *facile*) 478–85: no life is so short that a man cannot find time to die; however close death is, it is noble to kill oneself in an extremity.

b. (*necesse*) 485–7: you have no other choice than to die: then welcome death.

c. (*gloriosum*) 488–97: such a death will be glorious and conspicuous.

d. (*pium*) 497–504: by dying in this way you will surpass all other records of military devotion:[2] it is the least you can do to prove your loyalty to Caesar.

B. *Ab hostibus.*

e. (*forte*) 505–7: the enemy must know that we are indomitable, and they must fear our spirit.

f. (*honestum*) 507–14: it would be disgraceful to accept their offers of a compromise: such offers should serve only to increase our glory and to be a foil to our *virtus.*

---

[1] See Sen., *Ep.* 77. 6 for a brief suasoria on suicide: full references for the subject given by Summers, *Select Letters of Seneca* (London, 1940), 252–4.

[2] Lucan might have been expected to put in a list of *exempla* at this point. Cf. Sen., *Suas.* 6. 8: 'hoc loco hominum, qui ultro mortem apprehendissent, exempla posuit.'

Conclusio. 514–20.

My own mind is made up: I am irrevocably resolved to die. Already I am possessed by the wish for death and know what a blessing death is.

This is a rousing oration: Lucan introduces it by saying that Vulteius stiffened his men's resolve (474–5), and at the end he remarks that all his men were fired with a new courage (520–1), taking Bentley's conjecture *mobilium*). The effect is achieved by a straightforward *color*: the first word of the speech refers to Liberty, and death is seen as the brave man's only escape when his liberty is threatened. The style is forthright: there is no equivocation and Vulteius makes his points in a series of clearly-defined short sentences. Of the figures, much the most important are the *sententiae*:[1] the accumulation of these at either end of the speech (five in the first 12 lines, three in the last 18) is remarkable, and bears out Quintilian's statement that one should work on the emotions of the hearers particularly at these places (Quint. 6. 1, 52). Indeed, the speech is an outstanding example of Lucan's declamatory style.

2. Luc. 9. 379–406. *Cato's speech in the desert.*

The theme of this speech is summarized in 402–3:

> . . . serpens, sitis, ardor harenae
> dulcia virtuti: gaudet patientia duris.

The *color* is given in the opening lines—the crossing of the desert is to be the proving of the army's *virtus*: only in this way can true patriots recover Rome's liberty—*durum iter ad leges.*[2] The only alternative to liberty is death (380: *indomita cervice mori*): the sufferings that must be endured should be welcomed as a cause for joy. Even Heitland admits that the speech (down to 394) is 'very good': it is again noticeable that here, as in the panegyric on Pompey, the style becomes more flashy when Cato turns to speak of himself. Even so, the speech as a whole is impressive, a worthy summons by the great Stoic to his disciples to share in the proving of his *virtus*. The scheme is as follows:

Exordium. 379–81.

You have chosen to follow me as the only way to safety, preferring death to capitulation. Consider now the hardships that Virtue must endure.

---

[1] At 478–9; 479–80; 481–2 (expanded in 482–4); 484–5 (cf. 9. 211); 487; 503–4; 512–14; 517–20 (cf. 8. 632).

[2] Wrongly taken by Duff (Loeb ed.) as 'hard to win the love of our country in her fall'. The genitive is objective—'hard it is to show love for one's country in her fall'.

Narratio. 382–8.

You will meet with drought, heat, deserts and serpents: this is the hard way to liberty by which the patriot must be content to go.

Tractatio. 388–404.

a. (*honestum*) 388–92: I will not conceal the dangers; for only those who face them willingly can be of my band. Such endurance is noble and worthy of Romans.

b. (*generosum*) 392–4: those who choose the easy path and avoid danger deserve to live under a tyrant.[1]

c. (*forte*) 394–402: I shall lead you and share every hardship: where there is danger I shall be the first to face it; where comfort, I shall be the last to enjoy it.

d. (*iucundum*) 402–4: all the perils of the desert should be welcomed by the virtuous man. Virtue brings greater happiness when it is gained by suffering.

Conclusio. 405–6.

Only the dangers of Africa are sufficient to show that it was not cowardice that made you flee at Pharsalia—for Pharsalia was far less dangerous.

The first part of the speech is simpler than the later part (from 394), where the *sententiae* are sometimes very compressed. Thus the point in 398–401 must be inferred that Cato will be the last to drink (etc.), so that there will be no one else to be thirsty, hot or footsore. The repetition of the idea in 401–2, although neat in itself, does not clarify the point. Again, at 405–6, it requires some ingenuity to see that the point implied is that to flee from Pharsalia to Africa is to flee from one set of evils to something far worse. Yet this *sententia* is an adequate close to the speech, with *viros* as the final and emphatic word, preceded by the paradox of *deceat fugisse*.[2]

C. JUDICIAL

There is no clear example of this type in Lucan. However, the context of 9. 1014–32 makes the speech of the Egyptian courtier approximate to an advocate's speech: Caesar is in the position of a

---

[1] 'The tyrant' possibly: Duff's 'a master' is too weak.

[2] Other *sententiae* at 385; 402; 403; 404. Other figures used are *adiectio*—381; 382; 386; 388–9; with repetition (i.e. *anaphora*) 387–8; 398–9; with *tricolon* (Quint. 9. 3. 48 and 77; 398–401; 402–4: *alliteration*—379; 380; 384; 391; 392; 395; 400; 402: *emphasis*—392 (Romanum); 394 (dominum); 406 (deceat; viros): *hypallage*—384 (squalent serpentibus arva): *synedoche*—385 (leges *for* rem publicam liberam); 404–5 (virtuti, patientia, honestum—abstract for concrete).

judge, able to accept or reject; and the courtier, as Lucan says (1013), *commendat crimina*. Quintilian quotes the scene as an example of a compromise between deliberative and controversial speeches (3. 8, 55–8):

> solent in scholis fingi materiae ad deliberandum similiores controversiis et ex utroque genere commixtae, ut cum apud C. Caesarem consultatio de poena Theodoti ponitur. constat enim accusatione et defensione causa eius, quod est iudicialium proprium. permixta tamen est et utilitatis ratio, an pro Caesare fuerit occidi Pompeium, an timendum a rege bellum, si Theodotus sit occisus, an id minime opportunum hoc tempore et periculosum et certe longum sit futurum. quaeritur et de honesto, deceatne Caesarem ultio Pompeii, an sit verendum, ne peiorem faciat suarum partium causam, si Pompeium indignum morte fateatur. quod genus accidere etiam veritati potest. (Cf. Quint. 7. 2, 6.)

It is obvious that the whole scene in Lucan (9. 1010–1104), with the speeches of the courtier and of Caesar, is derived from the schools, and it must be admitted that the speeches in places read more like a student's exercise than Lucan's best rhetoric. The courtier's speech is of the *genus iudiciale* in that it contains the fivefold division and consists in part of a defence of the murder. On the other hand, as Quintilian says, the questions of *utile* and *honestum* enter in, which are properly the province of deliberative speeches. The way in which the first part of the *argumenta* is put (1022–6), with the verbs in the imperative mood, again belongs to the Suasoria. Analysis follows:

Exordium. 1014–18.

Caesar, you have conquered the world and Ptolemy has now completed your task for you.

Narratio. 1018–21.

We have killed Pompey; this is the price we are paying you for your friendship.

Probatio 1022–6.

(*utile*) by condoning the deed you will get control of Egypt: worthy will be the ally who dealt with Pompey in such a way.

Refutatio 1026–9.

(*magnum*) do not think our deed worthless: to do it we had to disregard our ancient friendship and obligations towards Pompey.

Peroratio. 1029–32.

Call the deed what you will; but if you call it a crime, the greater will be your debt to us for accepting the guilt ourselves.

The *color* of the speech is that the deed is one whose expediency far outweighs moral consideration. Among the tropes and figures, the figure *Irony* is important. At 1024–6 Lucan's implication is that Caesar is a suitable leader for the man who murdered Caesar's son-in-law: the superficial meaning is that so great a deed makes Ptolemy an ally worth having: he is like a freedman found indispensable to a household (emphasis here on *clientem* in 1024) because he has power over a member of it. At 1028–9 the superficial meaning is that to kill a man who has performed the good services mentioned (and has ties of *hospitium* derived from the previous generation) required a great moral effort, although the deed itself was easy enough: the inference is that it was the blackest of crimes.[1] All in all, however, the speech is too clever and the speaker too nasty to carry conviction: and perhaps this was Lucan's intention.

In these five passages, then, we have seen how Lucan applied the rules of declamation, which he had learned in the schools, to the craft of poetry. We are now in a position to examine certain themes which were common to declamation and epic poetry, and to see how Lucan's training in the one field affected his development in the other. Since this chapter has ended with Caesar in Egypt, it is natural to examine first the subject which Lucan associates with this episode— the tyrant Alexander.

[1] Among other figures are *adiectio*—1020–1; 1022–3; 1022–4 (*tricolon*, also involving *climax*— Quint. 9. 3, 54—and *anaphora*): 1031–2; *alliteration*—1016 (with assonance of—*ell*); 1019; 1024; 1024–5: *antonomasia*—1014 (terrarum domitor; Romanae maxime gentis); 1016 (rex Pellaeus); 1019, 1024 (Magnus); 1022 (regna Phari); 1023 (Niliaci gurgitis); 1026 (generum); 028 (parenti): *metonymy* —1017; 1019.

CHAPTER II

LUCAN AND ALEXANDER THE GREAT

BOOK 9 had closed with Caesar on board ship in the harbour of Alexandria refusing to approve of the murder of Pompey: his reaction to the offering of Pompey's head and the speech of the courtier was one of anger and sorrow, emotions which fooled neither Caesar's audience nor Lucan—*nec turba querenti credidit* (9. 1105-6). The next book opens with his landing in Egypt and visit to the tomb of Alexander;[1] but neither the visit nor Caesar's reactions are described by Lucan. Caesar, he tells us, made a rapid tour of the sights of the city; ignoring the usual attractions, he eagerly went down into the vault of Alexander's tomb (10. 14-19). There follows a denunciation of Alexander before the main story is resumed (at 53) with the introduction of Ptolemy and Cleopatra.

The denunciation (20-52), full of vigour and venom, is a declaimer's *locus*, and the extant declamations on Alexander, with the literary tradition of the philosophers and historians, illustrate Lucan's sources and methods. Lucan, however, by the time he came to compose the tenth book, had sufficient mastery of his epic material to be able to insert such a *locus* where it could best be integral to the structure of the poem. That it is to be thought of in this light, rather than as a digression, can be shown by consideration of its threefold relationship—to the structure of the epic, to its underlying theme, and to the character of Caesar.

The double catastrophe of Pharsalia and the subsequent murder of Pompey occupy books 7 and 8; a new phase, of the poem as of the Civil War, begins with book 9, heralded by the apotheosis of Pompey and the transference of his soul to Cato and Brutus (9. 1-18); the book is therefore largely devoted to Cato, the new guide of the Republic (9. 24-5—*patriam tutore carentem excepit*) and champion of Liberty (29-30). The principal episode of the book is the march across the Libyan desert, with the visit to the oracle of Jupiter Hammon and the encounter with the serpents. By this means Lucan presents Cato to his readers in the round: up to this

---

[1] The tomb has already been mentioned at 9. 153-4, where Gnaeus Pompeius by his threats draws the pathetic contrast between the honourable treatment of Alexander's body and the shameful neglect of his father's corpse.

13

point he has been more of a principle than a person (as in 2. 234–391), whereas in book 9 his character as patriot and leader is unfolded in the speeches and is seen objectively in his actions in rallying and leading the Pompeian survivors, above all in the desert march. The theme of the book is Cato's *virtus*, and its climax is the proving of his *virtus* in the desert. Lucan's symbolism is overt: the shipwreck on the Syrtes (319–47), the march from the barren east to the rich west (420–1), the conquest of serpents, desert-heat and thirst (402)— all constitute an allegory of Cato from the wreck of the Pompeian cause at Pharsalia, through the *durum iter ad leges* (385), to his conquest of adversity that is a triumph greater than any military glory (596–604).

The disaster at Pharsalia meant that Rome must be rebuilt: for Lucan the alternatives were a restoration of the Republic or a monarchy. The ἀριστεία of Cato presents the case for the first alternative; at 9. 950 attention is turned to Caesar, who embodies the second. Cato had crossed the desert as the symbol of his search for the new Rome; for Caesar the visit to Troy (9. 950–99) is equally symbolic. Around him lie the hidden ruins (966–9) of the proud city; the place is full of associations with her heroes and heroines. Caesar's thoughts dwell not on the past but on the future, when a new city will rise, the glory of Italy and of the descendants of Trojan Iulus: he prays to the Lares of Troy, to the spirits of her dead and to Pallas Athene (990–9):

> . . . date felices in cetera cursus,
> restituam populos; grata vice moenia reddent
> Ausonidae Phrygibus, Romanaque Pergama surgent.[1]

Lucan can now bring Caesar to Egypt and develop the next phase of the epic; it is a fair guess that this stage would have closed with the battle of Thapsus and the death of Cato. One might have expected book 10 to start with Caesar's arrival off Egypt and his first dealings with the Egyptian traitors; instead, the episode of Pompey's head is in book 9, and book 10 begins with the denunciation of Alexander. Lucan is right: in the first place, book 9 needs to end, as it had started, with the dead Pompey. Secondly, the squalor and hypocrisy of the closing episode contrast violently with the *virtus* of Cato. Thirdly, the denunciation is the more effective for being placed at the opening of a new book.

---

[1] The significance of this stage in the epic is further marked by Lucan's apostrophe (980–6) linking his poem to the *Iliad*.

As has been shown above, the alternative (after Pharsalia) to a Catonian republic was Caesarian monarchy: the *color* with which the two protagonists are to be presented is all-important. The key element in the unfavourable treatment of Caesar is his boundless ambition, his desire for dominion of the world. So long as Pompey was alive there was a chance that Caesar would be content with the position of *princeps*, sole leader in a republic in which his peers, too, were men of authority.[1] That possibility passed away with Pharsalia and the murder of Pompey; another phase of Caesar's ambition was revealed, to be sole master. Here we are at the heart of Lucan's poem; its theme is the destruction of Roman liberty by Civil War, the replacement of *Libertas* by *regnum*, of the magistrates by a *dominus*. Just as Lucan's own disillusionment with the rule of Nero is reflected in the growing republicanism of the poem, so is the fading hope (during the Civil War) of a restored republic reflected in his handling of the story and the characterization of Caesar. Caesar's will is to be no less than tyrant, and from his landing in Egypt all his energies will be concentrated on this end—*nulla captus dulcedine rerum* (10. 17).

Such is the context of the Alexander-denunciation. In the development of the epic it heralds a new chapter in the downfall of the Roman Republic; it is as relevant to the portrait of Caesar, for the denunciation of the man who imposed his sole will upon the world applies all too clearly to the Roman tyrant as he seeks to satisfy his ambition;[2] Caesar belongs to the same class as the tyrant Alexander. And it is the most sustained and explicit attack in the poem upon a tyrant:[3] it is here that Lucan's bitterness against the realities of Caesarism and Neronian autocracy derives strength from that imaginary figure, the declaimers' tyrant.

Few, if any, historical examples could be found of the heartless and bloodthirsty monsters of the declamations: Alexander was too explosive a phenomenon to be ignored, and the facts of his career provided ample ammunition for a *locus* on tyranny. No quarter can be expected for him in the schools. Equally unfavourable is his treatment at the hands of the philosophers, who never forgave his

[1] It is doubtful if Lucan could have shared this view—see 1. 146–50; 2. 227–32.
[2] For example, the metaphors in 10. 34–6 of *fulmen* and *sidus iniquum* allude to Caesar: for the former, cf. Luc. 1. 151–7, for the latter, Sen., *Cons. ad Marc.* 18. 3.
[3] The most important passages on the subject elsewhere in the poem are 1. 670; 2. 225–32; 7. 426–45; 9. 206–7. There are very many references to *regnum* and the loss of liberty—e.g. 1. 4, 86, 672; 4. 808–9; 7. 580–1, 602–3; 9. 96–7, 257, 392–4.

murder of Callisthenes.[1] According to the Peripatetics, Alexander (with Aristotle as his tutor) made a good start, but later (after the death of Darius) deteriorated; blinded by success, he became a cruel tyrant. He would indeed have come to a disastrous end, had not his Fortune saved him. This is substantially the portrait of Curtius, and it goes back to Theophrastus who, according to Cicero, was distressed by Alexander's prosperity (Cic., *T.D.* 3. 21). Theophrastus was further said to have quoted Chaeremon's line τύχη τὰ θνητῶν πράγματ' οὐκ εὐβουλία in his *Callisthenes* (Cic., *T.D.* 5. 25): τύχη was a distinctive and important feature of the Peripatetic portrait, although it is not always clear whether Fortune in general is meant, or Alexander's own particular Fortune.

To the Stoics, Alexander was bad from the start, and his tutor, Leonidas, was to be blamed for not having eradicated his pride (cf. Clem. Alex., 1. 7; Quint, 1. 1, 9): according to Seneca, Aristotle could not remove Alexander's *feritas* (*De Ira* 3. 17. 2): to Cicero he was proud and cruel (*Att.* 13. 28, 3) and lacked the *facilitas* and *humanitas* of his father: Seneca, further, calls him mad, lacking in self-control, immeasurably proud.[2]

The historians are a little less unkind: Diodorus is inconsistent but partly favourable;[3] Trogus emphasized Alexander's ambition to conquer the whole world.[4] There is, however, no evidence that Lucan consulted these authors. Livy is a different matter and there can be no doubt of his importance for Lucan.[5] In Livy, 9. 17–19, there is a digression on Alexander, where he considers what would have happened if Alexander had invaded Europe rather than Asia. He allows that Alexander was an excellent general, but in general his view is that of the Peripatetics: Alexander was lucky to die before his Fortune changed, while he was 'in incremento rerum'. After the conquest of Darius he became proud (instanced by his dress and his demand for προσκύνησις and adulation from his court) and vain (*vanitatem ementiendae stirpis*); he lost his moderation and gave way to anger and drunkenness. Even granting that he was undefeated, one must remember that there was little time for his Fortune to

---

[1] Cf. Sen., *N.Q.* 6. 23, 1–3: 'Alexandri crimen aeternum quod nulla virtus . . . redimet. For the literary portrait of Alexander see W. W. Tarn, *Alexander the Great* (Cambridge, 1948), vol. 1, 80–2; vol. 2, F, G, H and App. 16: *id.* 'Alexander, Cynics and Stoics', *A.J.P.* 60 (1939), 51–6. Also J. Stroux, 'Die Stoische Beurteilung Alex. d. Gr.', *Philologus* 88 (1933), 222, superseding W. Hoffmann, *Das literarische Porträt Alex. d. Gr.* (Leipzig, 1907).

[2] Sen., *Ben.* 2. 16. 1–2; 5. 6, 1: *Ep.* 91. 17; 94. 61–3.

[3] See Tarn, vol. 2, F.

[4] Justin, 11. 6, 3; 12. 13, 1–3: cf. Sen., *Ben.* 7. 2, 6–7; 7. 3, 1: *Ep.* 91. 17; 94. 62; 119. 7: *N.Q.* 5. 18, 9.

[5] See R. Pichon, *Les Sources de Lucain* (Paris, 1912), ch. 2.

change: the Romans of that day, then (Livy concludes), could easily
have proved themselves Alexander's equals, and their army would
have been a match for Alexander's; for the Macedonians depended
for success upon one man, while the Romans had many leaders,
each of whom was Alexander's equal. The digression ends with a
prayer for *concordia civilis*.

Here we are getting closer to Lucan: a survey of the Senecan
declamations on Alexander will complete the evidence necessary for
an understanding of the elements of his denunciation. Two *Suasoriae*
dealt with Alexander, 1 (*An Oceanum naviget*) and 4 (*An Babylona
intret*). The latter gave declaimers an opportunity to work in *loci*
on knowledge of the future and astrology: Seneca's quotations have
comparatively little bearing on Alexander. There are two relevant
sententiae however; 'Magnus iste et supra humanae sortis habitum
sit cui liceat terrere Alexandrum' finds an echo in the younger
Seneca (*Ben.* 5. 6, 1): 'Babylon ei cluditur cui patuit Oceanus?'
brings us back to the favourite target of the Stoics, Alexander's
ambition to conquer the world and sail the eastern ocean. *Suasoria*
1 is on this subject: there are vivid descriptions of Ocean (e.g. sect. 1:
cf. Curt. 9. 4, 18) and ingenious epigrams and paradoxes (e.g.
'Alexander orbi magnus est, Alexandro orbis angustus est', sect. 3).
Cestius (sect. 5) said that this *suasoria* would have to be spoken in a
different manner before a tyrant from that suitable to a free state,
and that some kings were less fond of truth than others, Alexander
being an example of one who was intolerably arrogant. Indeed,
says Seneca, the *suasoria* itself proves his arrogance, for he cannot be
satisfied with the world to which he belongs. The declaimers, then
use a *color* hostile to Alexander, in which his ambition to reach the
limits of the world is a prominent feature.

Thus the elements of Lucan's denunciation appear: Alexander
was mad, a tyrant and murderer, consumed with insatiable ambi-
tion, saved by his Fortune from a disastrous end. Analysis of the
passage will make this clear:

Exordium (20–28):

Alexander was a bandit,[1] who destroyed the liberty of much of
the world. He was mad:[2] yet he was spared full retribution,

---

[1] *Felix praedo* (21) in contrast to *non felix* at 51. Perhaps Lucan intends an allusion to Sulla
Felix in this reference to Alexander's Fortune.
[2] *vaesanus* (20, 42). Cf. Sen., *Suas.* 1. 9 (Fabianus): 'illa demum est magna felicitas quae
arbitrio suo constitit': *Suas.* 1. 3 (Albucius): 'magni pectoris est inter secunda moderatio.' Cf.
Cic., *T.D.* 5. 36. The man who cannot practise *moderatio*, according to the Stoics, is mad;
cf. Pers., *Sat.* 3. 116–18.

although his death was a just punishment, for his body should have
been torn apart and scattered over the world, a reminder of tyranny.

Tractatio (28–45):

(i) 28–36: Alexander's career summarized, his *furor* exemplified.
He left Greece and slaughtered the peoples of Asia, staining Euphrates
and Ganges with the blood of Persians and Indians.

(ii) 36–45: in his madness he planned to sail upon Ocean itself:
he was prepared to march round the world from East to West, from
North to South. But death put that limit to his ambition which
the world could not:[1] even then such was his *invidia* that, rather than
leave his empire for another to rule, he left it to be torn apart.

Peroratio (46–52):

Three *sententiae* working up to the final paradox:

1. 46: sed cecidit Babylone sua Parthoque verendus—

He died in Parthian Babylon, part of his empire.

2. 47–8: pro pudor! Eoi propius timuere sarisas
    quam nunc pila timent populi.

Even Alexander's success is shameful to Rome, whose legions
defeated the Macedonian phalanx, but cannot defeat the Parthians.

3. 48–51: . . . licet usque sub Arcton
    regnemus . . . cedemus in ortus
    Arsacidum domino.

Rome can conquer the North, West and South; but she cannot
equal Alexander's eastern conquests.

Final Paradox

(51–2): non felix Parthia Crassis
    exiguae secura fuit provincia Pellae.[2]

Lucan's Alexander, then, is drawn from the declaimers and
philosophers: the *color* of the denunciation is most conveniently
summed up by the words *vaesano regi* (42)—words which Lucan

---

[1] 'Occurrit suprema dies, naturaque solum / hunc potuit finem vaesano ponere regi.' Cf.
Suas. 1. 1: 'Haec est, Alexander, rerum natura: post omnia Oceanus, post Oceanum nihil.'
But at 3. 233–4 Lucan takes a different view: 'hic ubi Pellaeus post Tethyos aequora ductor /
constitit et magno vinci se fassus ab orbe est.' The scholiast on this passage says: 'Alexander
Magnus, cum Oceanum pernavigare vellet, subito vocis sonitu monitus est "Desiste".' Cf.
Suas. 1. 2.

[2] Note the symmetry of the final line. Among the figures in the passage may be noted
alliteration and *assonance* (20; 33; 35; 40; 52): *antithesis* (27; 47–8; 51–2): *antonomasia* (20; 42;
51—all for Alexander; 52, *Pellae*, is better taken as an ex. of *synecdoche*, part (Pella) for the
whole Macedonia)): *homoeoteleuton* (31–2; 40): *hyperbole* (31–3; 34; 39–40; 41–2): *sententia*
(25–8; 34–6; 46; 47–8; 48–51; 51–2).

would not hesitate to use of Caesar. The real object of the denuncia-
tion is Caesar, whose ambition has led to the destruction of the
Roman Republic in intestinal warfare. And so it is Livy who has
the clearest influence at the close: it is not to Alexander that Lucan
refers in the final paradox, but to the military might of Rome.
Livy had prayed that civil war might be averted: Lucan invokes the
name of Crassus, whose death at Carrhae removed the last obstacle
to the outbreak of the war that destroyed the liberty of Rome.[1]

We have shown that the denunciation of Alexander the Great
applies to Caesar: a common rhetorical theme has been used by
Lucan to give the *color* needed for his characterization of Caesar—in
this case Caesar, the *vaesanus rex*. Another case where the schools of
declamation provide a theme whose *color* fills out the portrait of
Caesar is the storm, by means of which Caesar is to be shown as
full of ὕβρις, for the moment the equal and favourite (he supposes)
of Fortune, but in reality saved for a terrible end. In the next two
chapters we shall first consider the place of the storm in Roman
literature and rhetoric and relate Lucan's storm-writing to the tradi-
tion, and then go on to analyse Caesar's storm as well as the other
storm-passages and related similes which feature so prominently in
the epic.

[1] See Luc. 1. 99–100: ' . . . nam sola futuri / Crassus erat belli medius mora' and 1. 106:
'Parthica Romanos solverunt damna furores.'

CHAPTER III

THE LITERARY BACKGROUND TO LUCAN'S STORMS

STORMS are parts of the furniture of Epic, an important feature of what Pliny called the *poetica descriptionum necessitas*. Lucan has no less than four storms, as well as a large number of storm-similes and incidental references:[1] his critics have taken particular delight in attacking the great storm in Book 5,[2] and few are prepared to see any purpose in it other than sheer love of rhetorical display. In the present chapter a survey will be made of the literary tradition of storm-writing: such a survey, it is true, will take us far from Lucan; but it is necessary if we are to set his storms in their proper perspective. In any case, the material for a study of the subject is not easily accessible, while a full consideration of Lucan's storms and their predecessors is overdue.[3] The following chapter will provide detailed analysis of the storms as well as considerations of the similes.

The Literary Tradition

The sea was so much part of Greek life that it is surprising that descriptions of storms do not enter more into Greek literature: perhaps the Greeks had less time to be spectators of the scene, occupied as they were in the business of seafaring. To Hesiod (*W & D* 617–95) the sea is something evil: to Homer and the tragedians it is hostile, but to be accepted and faced. In mythology storms are prominent in the wanderings of Odysseus and the return of Agamemnon. Homer's storms provided the elements of all that followed, while their directness and simplicity ensured that any imitation could only be for the worse. In the first storm (*Od.* 5. 291 sqq.), Poseidon gathers the clouds and raises the sea with his trident; the four cardinal winds all blow together. Odysseus reflects on his plight and wishes that he had died at Troy, where at least he could have had an

---

[1] The storms are at 4. 48–120; 5. 504–677; 9. 319–47; 9. 445–92.

[2] e.g. Heitland (Haskins' ed., lxxvii): '. . . and so on, till the resources of absurdity are exhausted.'

[3] The main work for the subject is E. de St. Denis, *Le Rôle de la Mer dans la Poèsie Latine* (Paris, 1935): it incorporates the work of C. Liedloff, *De Tempestatis . . . Descriptionibus . . .* (Leipzig, 1884). See also W.-H. Friedrich, 'Episches Unwetter', *Festschr. B. Snell*, Munich 1956, 77–87: U. Piacentini, *Osservazioni sulla Tecnica Epica di Lucano* (Berlin, 1963), 27–33. For similes, see J. Aymard, *Quelques Séries de Comparaisons chez Lucain* (Montpelier, 1951).

honourable burial:[1] his speech is interrupted by a great wave which hurls him from the raft and brings down the mast and tackle; while he struggles in the water, the raft disintegrates. He is only saved by divine intervention, first of Ino, then of Athena, who allows only one wind (Boreas) to blow; this it does for two nights and days, until Odysseus is brought close to Phaeacia, where he eventually lands with further help from Athena. In the second storm (*Od.* 12. 403–25), which is raised by Zeus, darkness is the dominant feature; a violent gust from the west brings down the ship's tackle, killing the helmsman; this is followed by thunder and lightning, which hurls the sailors overboard to be drowned (418–19: cf. Virg., *Aen.* 1. 118), except for Odysseus, who only falls into the sea when the ship breaks apart. Supported on timbers he drifts back to Scylla and Charybdis, blown thither by the south wind, which has taken the place of the west wind (426–7: cf. Luc., 2. 454–60).

Here are the elements of the literary storm, recurring throughout ancient literature: winds either blowing all together (i.e. a cyclone) or singly (hurricane), high seas with one wave bigger than the rest, darkness, clouds, thunder and lightning; disintegration of the vessel, despair and (generally) death of the sailors.

The Agamemnon story introduces a new feature: Odysseus was the much-enduring hero pursued by the hostility of certain gods, but Ajax Oileus had committed sacrilege before the altar of Athena and added blasphemy to this by boasting (after the shipwreck) that the gods could not kill him. For this he was killed by a thunderbolt launched either by Poseidon (*Od.* 4. 505–10) or Athena (*Aen.* 1. 42–5: cf. Eur., *Tro.* 80). The storm and death of Ajax were described in the *Nostoi* of the Epic Cycle:[2] of the extant authors, Euripides (*Tro.* 77–81) referred to the death of Ajax, Aeschylus (*Ag.* 649–57) and Sophocles (in his *Teucer*: cf. frag. 507, Dindorf) to the storm raised by Athena. Sophocles' storm must have been colourful, to judge from Pacuvius' adaptation (in his *Teucer*, quoted below, p. 24) and famous, if Aristophanes could incorporate a quotation from it in his *Clouds* (583). Aeschylus' description, involving the main Homeric features, is compressed; it emphasizes the collision of the

---

[1] 311–12: cf. *Il.* 21. 281; Aesch., *Cho.* 351–3, 363 sqq.: Virg., *Aen.* 1. 94: Ovid, *Tr.* 1. 2. 51–6; *Met.* 11. 539–40; *Fast.* 3. 597–8; Sen., *N.Q.* 5. 18, 5: Pliny, *N.H.* 19. 6. In Ennius, Thyestes' oath begins *ut naufragio pereat Atreus* (*R.O.L.* 1. 366), upon which Cicero (*T.D.* 1. 44. 107) remarked: 'durum hoc sane; talis enim interitus non est sine gravi sensu.'

[2] Proclus (O.C.T. ed. of Homer, vol. 5, p. 108): εἶθ' ὁ περὶ τὰς Καφηρίδας πέτρας δηλοῦται χειμὼν καὶ ἡ Αἴαντος φθορά.

disorganized ships and contains the notorious metaphor of the sea 'sprouting' (ἀνθοῦν) corpses.

There are no other full-scale storm-passages extant in fifth-century tragedians: Euripides evidently had a rainstorm at the end of his *Alcmene*,[1] and his description of the wave which brought the sea-monster to the shore at Troezen (*Hipp.* 1201–12: cf. Hom., *Il.* 15. 624–9) is related to storm-passages. In particular, the hyperbole of the mountains being hidden from view by the wave found its way into Silver Latin descriptions.[2] Sophocles has a moving storm-simile in the *Antigone*[3] as well as a compressed and vivid description of a dust-storm (*Ant.* 415–21). In later Greek literature there is a major storm in Apollonius (2. 1108–1121), which would, presumably, have appeared in Varro's translation: it is derivative from Homer (*Od.* 12. 403 sqq., especially) and adds no new details.[4]

There was little that Roman poets could add to the Greek tradition, as far as mere description went. It is not surprising to find Seneca (Rhetor) saying, of the generation after Virgil, that their descriptions of Ocean were inclined to be feeble—either sketchy or too detailed (*Suas.* 1. 15). He then goes on to quote a vigorous hexameter passage by Albinovanus Pedo, which owes its excellence to the fact that it was inspired by new discoveries and a new attitude to the sea and its storms. It was the excitement of fresh explorations that had inspired Homer's treatment of the sea; something of the same dynamic influence gave the impulse to the early Roman poets, after the Punic wars and Rome's conquest of the sea. This is why they and their successors (down to Virgil) could adapt their Greek models with such freshness and imagination. The *Pax Augusta* opened a new age for Roman seafaring, and the extension of the Empire and trade should have inspired a fresh approach in Roman marine writing: yet the first century (A.D.) could produce nothing greater than a Seneca or a Lucan. And so the descriptive tradition ran to its end in the entirely derivative storms of Silius (12. 603; 17. 237), Statius (*Theb.* 5. 363) and Valerius Flaccus (1. 574). Even

---

[1] Plautus, *Rud.* 86: 'non ventus fuit, verum Alcumena Euripidi'. See E. A. Sonnenschein, 'Alcumena Euripidi', *C.R.* 28 (1914), 40–1: A. S. Murray, 'The Alcmene Vase', *J.H.S.* 11 (1890), 225–30 and Pl. 6.

[2] Sen., *Phaedr.* 1008–30 (esp. 1014 and 1022–4): *Ag.* 471: Luc., 5. 615–16, 625.

[3] *Ant.* 584–92: a prosperous house overwhelmed by disaster is like the sea churned up by a gale. For churning up the sea-floor, cf. Virg., *Aen.* 1. 107; 3. 557: Ovid, *Met.* 11. 499; *Tr.* 1. 4. 6.: Sall., *Jug.* 80.

[4] The influence of Greek prose storms on Latin authors cannot be assessed. Herodotus' storms, at 7. 188–91; 8. 12–13, may be as much poetical as historical (see How and Wells' note on 7. 188. 1): Virg., *Aen.* 1. 119 may be a reminiscence of Hdt., 7. 190.

Tacitus, in his description of Germanicus' North Sea storm (*Ann.* 2. 23) could only reproduce the traditional features, without even considering the suitability of transferring a Mediterranean storm to the North Sea. Juvenal's sneer is a fitting epitaph to the descriptive tradition—*omnia fiunt | talia tam graviter siquando poetica surgit | tempestas.*[1]

We may now turn to an outline of the descriptive tradition in Roman storm-writing, of which Virgil was the culmination. This will be followed by an examination of new elements in the tradition, mainly scientific and philosophical, which were the Roman authors' contribution to the genre. These could have saved the Roman tradition from its fate at the hands of the rhetorical schools, and Lucan represents the last effort to reassert the strength of the 'new' approach. But he was himself the prisoner of his education, nor was his genius great enough to inspire a new tradition: his successors could only imitate and his fire, such as it was, was extinguished.

A. The Descriptive Tradition

Livius Andronicus was the first to bring the Greek storm into Latin poetry, particularly in his *Aegisthus* (which described Agamemnon's storm) and his translation of the *Odyssey*.[2] Naevius, however, appears to have been more influential, and it is to him that we should look for the beginnings of the Roman tradition. He was, according to Macrobius (*Sat.* 6. 2. 31), the main source for Virgil's storm in *Aen.* 1, although elsewhere (*Sat.* 5. 2. 13) Macrobius expressly quotes this storm as an example of Virgil being a 'mirror of Homer'. None of Naevius' storm is extant: only fragments from his *Danae* (*R.O.L.* 2, fr. 8) and a line quoted by the Scholiast on Lucan 6. 126 (*R.O.L.* 2, fr. 40) are connected with storm-phenomena.

Ennius provides more solid evidence. From the *Annales* a fine storm-simile survives:[3]

> concurrunt veluti venti quom spiritus Austri
> imbricitor Aquiloque suo cum flamine contra
> indu mari magno fluctus extollere certant.

---

[1] *Sat.* 12. 22–4: Juvenal's attitude to the sea may be summed up by 12. 81–2: 'gaudent . . . garrula securi narrare pericula nautae.'

[2] The only relevant extant line is fr. 18 (Hom., *Od.* 5. 297). Quotations and references for early Latin poetry are taken from E. H. Warmington's *Remains of Old Latin* (*R.O.L.*), 4 vols., London, 1936.

[3] *R.O.L.* 1. fr. 430–2 (quoted by Macr., *Sat.* 6. 2. 28): for *imbricitor* cf. Luc., 5. 608–9: cf. also Ennius, fr. 561 with Virg., *Aen.* 1. 51.

Here the battle of the winds makes its debut in the Latin hexameter; although the simile is taken from Homer, the Latin has a vigour and resonance, helped by alliteration and assonance, which give it a distinctive character. Elsewhere Ennius introduces *fremitus* of the sound of water (fr. 534–5: cf. Accius fr. 382, 393): his *qui caelum versat stellis fulgentibus aptum* (fr. 59) is used by Lucretius in the beautiful *Stellis fulgentibus apta | concutitur caeli domus* (6. 357–8).

The most famous of all early Latin storms is that of Pacuvius (*Teucer*, fr. 350–365), quoted with admiration by Cicero (*De Orat.* 3. 157; *Div.* I. 24). The extant fragments are given here. Teucer announces (fr. 341):

> periere Danai, plera pars pessum data est.

After some dialogue, the description itself follows:

... mihi classem imperat	350
Thessalum nostramque in altum ut properiter deducerem ...	
... Nerei repandirostrum incurvicervicum pecus.[1]	
... profectione laeti piscium lasciviam	
intuemur nec tuendi capere satietas potest.	
interea prope iam occidente sole inhorrescit mare	355
tenebrae conduplicantur, noctisque et nimbum obcaecat nigror.	
flamma inter nubes coruscat, caelum tonitru contremit,	
grando mixta imbri largifico subita praecipitans cadit,	
undique omnes venti erumpunt, saevi existunt turbines,	
fervit aestu pelagus ...	360
rapide retro citroque percito aestu praecipitem ratem	
reciprocare, undaeque e gremiis subiectare adfligere ...	
... armamentum stridor ...	
... flictus navium ...	
... strepitus fremitus clamor tonitruum et rudentum sibilus.	365

Here for the first time is the full apparatus of the Roman storm. First the description of the fair weather and its signs; then, as night falls, the sea grows rough, the darkness of night is made darker by the oncoming storm. There are clouds, thunder, lightning, hail and conflicting winds. The ships are tossed back and forth, up and down; the sails and rigging whistle and crack, the ships collide: most of the sailors are drowned. All these details can be found in Homer, Aeschylus or Sophocles: yet the Roman poet still has originality—his description is powerful for its sonorous compounds, the use of

---

[1] Quoted with disapproval by Quintilian, 1. 5. 67. It is a magnificently bombastic line, defying translation.

onomatopoeia, alliteration and assonance, the rugged rhythm. The literary storm was never to be the same again.[1]

Among the several fragments of Accius (the younger contemporary and friend of Pacuvius) describing storms and meteorological phenomena the most important are those from the *Clytemnestra*. Thus, in describing Agamemnon's storm, he says of the darkness (fr. 237–8): cf. Aesch., *Ag.* 649 sqq.) *deum regnator nocte caeca caelum e conspectu abstulit*: after the wreck, *flucti inmisericordes iacere, taetra ad saxa adlidere*. He puts more emphasis than Aeschylus on the fate of Ajax: his description was quoted by Cicero (*Top.* 16. 61) and at least once imitated by Virgil.[2] In the *Medea* of Accius a shepherd describes his first sight of a ship, the *Argo*, in terms of a storm or a vast tidal wave (fr. 381–94: Cic., *N.D.* 2. 35. 89). Accius uses bold alliteration: in the *Medea* man takes to the sea *ut tristis turbinum toleraret hiemes* (fr. 401–2); and equally striking effects are to be found at fr. 183–5 (sudden thunder), 571–2 (the North wind), 573–7 (waves breaking on the shore—triple alliteration of *c, l, s*). Yet there is a feeling that with Accius we are moving away from the power and freshness of Pacuvius, despite such flashes as *crispisulcans igneum fulmen* (fr. 239–240). The apparatus of the storm has been stabilized and description can only develop in the direction of greater detail. If the Roman storm was to stay alive it could not go further along this road, and it was fortunate that at this stage the genius of Lucretius appeared.

There are no set storm-passages in Lucretius—hardly surprising in one whose purpose was so different from that of his Roman predecessors. However, the first 534 lines of book 6 are devoted to τὰ Μετέωρα. Much the greater part of this section is concerned with the phenomena of the thunderstorm, in this reflecting (as Bailey in his edition, vol. 3, p. 1552, points out) 'the very large part lightning and thunder played in the whole system of omen and augury, which was a prominent element in Roman religion and indeed in Roman political and private life.' There are undoubtedly passages which influenced Virgil and his successors, while Lucretius still makes full use of the devices of his predecessors, such as the alliteration of *c* and *t*.[3] It was the range of his poetic imagination that brought new life to the subject, as can be seen by comparing the austerity of his original

---

[1] For Pacuvius' influence see: *Aen.* 1. 87 (Pac., fr. 363, 365); 9. 668 sqq. (358): Sen., *Ag.* 449–55; *Oed.* 466 (352–4); *Ag.* 472–4 (356); 474 sqq. (359–60); 494–5 (357); 498 (364).

[2] Fr. 241–2, said by Servius auct. to be the source of *Aen.* 1. 44.

[3] See, for example, Lucr., 6. 250–5; and cf. *Aen.* 3. 194–9; Lucan 5. 627–31; 1. 151–4.

(the *Letter to Pythocles*) with the richness of his own writing.[1] As an example of his contribution to the ideas of later poets one may take 6. 290–2, on the rain that follows thunder and lightning:

> quo de concussu sequitur gravis imber et uber,
> omnis uti videatur in imbrem vertier aether
> atque ita praecipitans ad diluviem revocare . . .

The idea of the Flood was a commonplace of Stoic authors, who owe this hyperbole for heavy rain to their Epicurean predecessor.[2]

The nearest that Lucretius comes to a *poetica tempestas* is at 1. 271–6, where he describes the force of the wind. There was no need for him to give so full a description if his purpose was merely to prove that the wind must be made up of particles of matter: he was the first to join poetic exuberance to the austerities of philosophical speculation, and it is not surprising that his meteorological passages influenced and enriched the storm-writing of his successors.[3]

And so the way was prepared for Virgil, whose storms are by far the most important single influence on the writing of his successors —indeed, not one of the set-piece storms of the silver age can be considered without reference to him. His achievement was in part to blend the storms of Homer with the Roman tradition: but his storms are purely literary—commentators from Seneca onwards have pointed out that he has transferred Homer's Adriatic storms to the western Mediterranean,[4] an inaccuracy that has increased the absurdity of some of Virgil's imitators.[5] Not surprisingly, Virgil is the watershed of the Roman storm-tradition: although the descriptive tradition continued to flourish, there was little that could be added. At this point, therefore, it is suitable to consider other elements in the development of Roman storm-writing before turning to the influence of the rhetorical schools which now became paramount.

B. PHILOSOPHICAL AND OTHER ELEMENTS IN THE TRADITION

a. *Physical speculation and didactic poetry*

One of the most popular subjects in Roman didactic writing (itself largely based on Greek originals) was meteorological phenomena.

---

[1] See Bailey's Lucretius ed., vol. 3, p. 1595, note 1.

[2] Cf. Lucan, 5. 620–4: Ovid, *Met.* 11. 516–18. The cataclysm is discussed below, pp. 47–9: the *locus classicus* is Sen., *N.Q.* 3. 27–8.

[3] E.g. *Aen.* 1. 59 (Lucr. 1. 277): Lucan 5. 595 (Lucr. 1. 294).

[4] Sen., *N.Q.* 5. 16, 2, quoting *Aen.* 1. 85–6 (cf. Tac., *Ann.* 2. 23 for a blatant example of transference). Virgil's storms are at *Aen.* 1. 34–158; 3. 192–208; 5. 8–34; also *Culex* 341–57. The first is the *locus classicus* for 'cyclonic', the second for 'black', the third for sudden storms. See St. Denis, 217–24.

[5] E.g. Milton, *P.R.* 4. 409–31: however, as Lucan said, *invidus qui vates ad vera vocat*.

According to Pliny (*N.H.* 2. 117) more than 20 Greek authors had written meteorological treatises: the tradition stretched back to the pre-Socratics, the most important of whom (from the point of view of his influence on Roman writing) was Empedocles: his work *On Nature* would have described the phenomena of the storm, although it is true that none of the surviving fragments do so.[1] Aristotle's *Meteorologica* crystallized the tradition and affected subsequent research; his work was continued by Theophrastus, much of whose *Weather-signs* can be found lurking in the first *Georgic*.[2] A parallel tradition stems from Eudoxus of Cnidos; its most important work is the *Phaenomena* of Aratus. This was immensely popular; the names of 27 commentators are known, and the work was translated into Latin by Cicero, Varro of Atax and Germanicus, of authors before Lucan's day. The *Diosemeia* (Prognostics) was particularly influential; whole sections were taken over by Virgil and from there found their way into Lucan. Many of the signs are reproduced by Pliny.[3] In the main body of the *Phaenomena* there is one digression on storms (408–35) and one epigram which was popular with Roman declaimers.[4]

A third Greek tradition was that of the philosophical schools. For the Epicureans, the *Letter to Pythocles* is important; for the Stoics the chief work is the Μετεωρολογικὴ Στοιχείωσις of Posidonius, which in its turn was the main source for Seneca's *Naturales Quaestiones*.[5]

Too few fragments remain of the *Epicharmus* of Ennius for us to be able to assess its influence on later Roman storm-writing. Of subsequent pre-Virgilian didactic poems those of Cicero and Lucretius are, of course, the most important. Lucretius first showed that it was possible to unite poetic imagery with scientific exposition; this is one of the distinguishing features of Lucan's storm-writing. Virgil's didactic method was, as Macrobius pointed out (*Sat.* 5. 16, 5),

[1] Empedocles frags. given in translation by J. Burnet, *Early Greek Philosophy* (ed. 4, London. 1930), 204–21. For Empedocles and Lucretius, see Bailey's ed. of Lucretius, vol. 1, Proleg. ii 2–3, pp. 25–9. I am aware that to pass from Empedocles to Aristotle is to omit much of importance, e.g. the work of Democritus.

[2] Fr. 6 in the Teubner text: the Loeb ed. (1916, A. Hort) is bound with the *Enquiry into Plants*: the Loeb ed. of Aratus quotes the parallel passages from Theophrastus.

[3] *N.H.* 18. 359–65.

[4] *Phaen.* 299: ὀλίγον 2ὲ 2ιὰ ξύλον 'ΑΪ2' ἐρύκει. Longinus, *De Subl.* 10. 5–6, compares with Hom., *Il.* 15. 624–8: for the epigram's probable origin (Anacharsis) see Diog. Laert., 1. 8, 5. It appears in Sen., *Contr.* 7. 1. 10; Sen., *Med.* 306–8: cf. Juv., *Sat.* 12. 57–9 14. 289.

[5] See Bailey, ed. of Lucretius, vol. 1, 25 sqq., and cf. Lucr., 6. 423–9 with Sen., *N.Q.* 5. 13. 3. For the influence of Posidonius on the climate of opinion at Rome with regard to the physical universe, see A. D. Nock, 'Posidonius', *J.R.S.* 49 (1959), 1–15 (esp. 12 sqq.).

the supreme example of mixing the brimstone with the treacle; hence his digression in the first *Georgic* (351 sqq.), which was copied by Lucan. Lucan started his great storm with a passage on weather-signs, and this would have been accepted and understood by his hearers, to such an extent had the framework of Epic altered by his day: to certain modern critics (e.g. Heitland, p. lxxv) the proper place for such a digression is a didactic poem, because this was the Virgilian canon. Such criticism may be aesthetically valid; but it ignores the conventions of epic in the Silver age.

Of didactic poems written between the time of Virgil and of Lucan one should mention the translation of Aratus made by Germanicus, the *Astronomicon* of Manilius and the *Aetna*. Manilius' work, being concerned with astrology, is found to influence Lucan particularly at the end of his first book, whereas references to meteorological phenomena were only incidental; only a few similarities have any bearing on storms.[1] The *Aetna* is concerned with terrestrial rather than celestial phenomena, and no certain connection can be established between it and Lucan. The similarity of subject-matter—for storms and volcanoes both show the power of Nature and cause upheavals in the normal course of things—does lead to similarities in vocabulary and ideas;[2] above all, the poem is evidence for the speculation on physical matters current in Lucan's day. This is true also of the passages in Pliny and Seneca that bear on the weather,[3] which bear many similarities to Lucan's facts (as opposed to his poetic colouring). It is impossible to say how far all these writers and the mass of scientific speculation influenced Lucan. It is abundantly clear that from the time of Lucretius to that of Lucan there flourished among educated Romans what A. D. Nock called 'a sense for the wonders of nature'. The wonders of nature were the poet's province, as Virgil (*Georg.* 2. 475–80) in a famous passage had said: it was the poet's right to use all the resources of his art to describe the phenomena of the weather, and Lucan's storm-scenes owe much to the vigorous spirit of inquiry and sense of wonder.

---

[1] See F. Schwemmler, *De Lucano Manilii Imitatore* (Leipzig, 1916): cf. Man. 5. 502 (496) and Luc. 1. 156–7: Man. 1. 168–70 and Luc. 9. 466–71: Man. 5. 744–5 and Luc. 1. 656–7.

[2] E.g. *Aet.* 199–207 and Luc. 5. 632–7: *Aet.* 236–7 and Luc. 5. 549 (both passages from Virg., *Georg.* 1. 427 sqq.): *Aet.* 379–84 and Luc. 5. 598 sqq. (cf. Sen., *N.Q.* 6. 18). See F. R. D. Goodyear's ed. (Cambridge, 1965), pp. 56–9, for a survey of evidence for date of *Aetna*.

[3] Pliny, *N.H.* 2. 117–34; 18. 340–65. Sen., *N.Q.* 1. 2. 5–10; 1. 6. 1–2; 1. 13. 2; 3. 27–30; 5, esp. 12–13, 16–18; 6. 9. 1.

b. *Moralizing*

The view that the sea is better left alone goes back to Hesiod: it flourished from the Augustan age onwards and was especially popular among Stoic moralizers, who found it a useful context for *loci* against avarice, luxury or travel.[1] Hesiod (*W & D.* 236-7) implies that seafaring is the result of an unjust and imperfect society: later (684-6) he says that men will risk the dangers of the sea through love of money. And death by drowning was for Hesiod worse than other ways of dying (687). These sentiments were echoed by Roman poets. For Virgil, seafaring was one of the signs of imperfection before the return of the Golden Age (*Ecl.* 4. 31-9): Ovid repeatedly expresses horror of death by drowning: 'at least', he says, 'it is something to die without being food for fishes' (*Tr.* 1. 2. 56).

In this tradition, then, seafaring was evidence of the imperfectness of man: it was, above all, an example of his *audacia*. This is Horace's theme, as it was that of the speakers in the first Senecan *Suasoria*; the sea was *Oceanus dissociabilis*, put there by the Creator to keep men apart (*Od.* 1. 3. 17-26). Horace, who had been in an Adriatic storm (*Od.* 3. 27. 18-20), was aware of the trappings of the literary storm (*Epod.* 10)—the battling winds, the waves beating on the boat from both sides, the broken oars, darkness, fear. These features, introduced not so much to display his art as incidentally or with an ironical touch, are the signs of the anger of the gods at human impiety in venturing on the sea. He denounces seafaring in his plea for a return to the old standards of simplicity and incorruptibility (*Od.* 1. 3. 35-41): in his perfect society, far beyond Ocean, there will be no seafaring, no trade, no Argo.[2]

The Argo, indeed, had long been a byword, and the opening of the *Medea* of Euripides was too well known not to be imitated;[3] 'Miseris tu gentibus, Argo, fata paras', says Valerius Flaccus (*Arg.* 1. 648-9). Seneca (*N.Q.* 5. 18. 3) debated whether the winds had brought more harm to men than good, with regard to the discovery of seafaring; he concluded that seafaring was not in itself a bad thing, but had been made so by men's perversion of it for purposes of war. Rather men should sail to discover more, to exchange ideas and goods. But the declaimers kept more closely to Horace's lead: 'aliena quid aequora remis / et sacras violamus aquas divumque

---

[1] E.g. Pliny, *N.H.* 2. 118: for Seneca, see A. Oltramare, *Les Origines de la Diatribe Romaine* (Lausanne, 1926), theme 81.

[2] *Epod.* 16. 41-2 and 57-8: cf. Virg., *Ecl.* 4. 34; Sen., *Med.* 301-79; Pliny, *N.H.* 19. 1-6. The sentiment is familiar from *Revelation*, 21. 1.

[3] E.g. Ennius, *R.O.L.* 1, fr. 253-61.

quietas / turbamus sedes?' asks Pedo (*Suas.* 1. 15. 29), and to most of the speakers in the first *Suasoria* crossing Ocean is another sign of Alexander's *hubris*—'ipsa suasoria insolentiam eius coarguit; orbis illum suus non capit' (*Suas.* 1. 5: cf. Luc. 10. 36–7). A stormy sea was suitable for tyrants and criminals: Haterius, having described a storm, draws the moral—*exspectat inquam, parricidam mare*.[1]

This has considerable bearing on Lucan and his great storm. Here was a case of supreme *audacia*, for Caesar was boldly tempting Fortune (5. 510, 591–3, 653–4). This was in line with his perverted qualities—'quo te, dure, tulit virtus temeraria?' cry his officers next day (5. 682). As Caesar sets out on his adventure, Fortune is his only companion (510): in the rising storm he disdains the power of the sea, for he knows that he is Fortune's favourite (578–93). At the climax of the storm he is at his most arrogant:

> . . . credit iam digna pericula Caesar
> Fatis esse suis. 'Quantusne evertere' dixit
> 'me superis labor est, parva quem puppe sedentem
> tam magno petiere mari?' (654–6)

He has no fear of death; he has achieved the full measure of his ambition—except for the throne, and of that disappointment only Fortune shares his knowledge (666–8). He has no need of a decent burial, for, god-like, he is ubiquitous, feared in every land (668–71).

It comes as something of an anticlimax, when we expect an end at least as dramatic as that of Ajax, that Caesar should be miraculously saved by a 'tenth wave' (672–7). The scene that follows owes much to the first *Suasoria*: its purpose is to contrast Caesar's attitude with that of his followers: he knows that he is the equal of Fortune; to them he is tempting a superior and dangerous power (692–5).

In examining this aspect of the storm we come near to the heart of the poem. Lucan has drawn from Horace and the moralizers the idea of the savage sea (which is implicit in all his seascapes, even when the sea is calm—*saeva quies pelagi* at 5. 442): only the *audaces* are not deterred from venturing upon it. From the schools he has drawn the idea of the Tyrant daring to sail upon Ocean; going with this is the concept of the *parricida* launched on the stormy sea in an inadequate vessel to vindicate his innocence (thus the title of Seneca, *Contr.* 7. 1). Caesar was indeed a *parricida*, the murderer (indirectly) of his son-in-law and of his fatherland, whose liberty he destroyed. In this Caesar and Cato are most significantly contrasted: Cato, true

---

[1] Sen., *Contr.* 7. 1. 4: cf. Pliny, *Paneg.* 34 and 35.

father of his fatherland (9. 601), faces danger as the trial of his *virtus*; Caesar provokes it to display his *superbia* and to prove that he is no less than the equal of Fortune herself. Lucan has taken the traditional commonplaces and transformed them to serve the purposes of his poem.

c. *The Spirit of Adventure*

The disapproval of the moralizers was confined to books and declamations: in real life, the Augustan age had ushered in a period of renewed interest in the sea, of expanded trade, of exploration. Just as the excitement of Greek marine discovery was reflected in the Odyssey, and the first achievement of sea power by the Romans in Naevius and the early Roman poets, so much of the writing from Virgil to Lucan reflects a vivid interest in the sea and its possibilities. This can be distinguished from the descriptions of the declaimers and commonplaces of the moralizers, which matched the taste of the rich men who, as Fabianus complained, had never seen the sea (Sen., *Contr.* 2. 1. 13). But those to whom the new voyages were material for epic, or who profited from the new opportunities for trade and power, could handle the commonplace so that it reflected something of the wonder felt by the Romans in the new discoveries. One such writer was Albinovanus Pedo, part of whose epic on the elder Germanicus' voyage in 12 B.C. was quoted by Seneca (Rhetor) as an example of a description that far excelled the declaimers (*Suas.* 1. 15): although Pedo is adopting the moralists' view, his vigorous lines cannot conceal the excitement of the discovery of the Northern seas with their unpredictable weather and strange monsters. Seneca the younger is another writer of this group: although he has long passages of commonplace writing on the sea and its storms, he can still write of the *vaga ponti mobilis unda* (*H.F.* 1056); he can approve of expanded trade and refer to the new horizons.[1] In fact, Claudius had had the *corona navalis* fixed to the gable of his palace after his British expedition as a sign of the conquest of Ocean (Suet., *Claud.* 17); he had introduced an insurance scheme for corn-merchants against storms (*ib.* 18), as well as offering rewards for those who built merchant-ships, such was his concern for the expansion of commerce. These were the attitudes and ideas current in Lucan's lifetime, and from them his own interest in the sea and its storms drew some of its strength.

[1] E.g. Germany (*Med.* 372–4); Red Sea (*Thy.* 371–3; *H.O.* 661–2); China (*Thy.* 379; *H.O.* 414). Cf. Luc., 1. 19–20.

C. Rhetorical Influence

All the literary storms subsequent to Virgil are stamped with his manner, for his work was a substantial part of the basic reading in the schools of declamation which became the training ground for poets. Ovid has five set storms, of which two are purely literary, while the three from the *Tristia* have some basis in personal experience.[1] St. Denis concludes that Ovid was the prisoner of rhetorical influence and incapable of appreciating the grandeur of the sea. It is true that most of his descriptions can be accounted for by the declaimers' storm-formulae (based on Virgil): yet even so, the most extended of the descriptions (in the *Metamorphoses*) has considerable power: it is clear that Lucan owed much to it.

Of Livy's two extant storms (21. 58. 3–11; 40. 58. 3–7), the more dramatic is that which occurs in the story of Hannibal's crossing the Apennines. The ingredients are familiar—wind, rain, 'twisters', thunder, the helplessness of the soldiers. But this was only the start, for Livy's storm, like those of Lucan and Virgil (at *Aen.* 1. 102), was divided into two parts. There followed stronger wind, lifting the rain and turning it into ice and hail which froze their victims to death. Undoubtedly Livy would have had a marine description in book 18 (the *Epitome* says 'res . . . prospere gestas deformaverunt naufragia classium'); while this is lost, we can see from Hannibal's mountain-storm that Livy follows the usual pattern of the literary storm. Petronius (*Sat.* 121; *Bell. Civile*, 196–208) used Livy's storm for his description of Caesar's crossing of the Alps in the winter of 50–49: Lucan limits his account of the same episode to a single line (1. 183)—it would have weakened the effect of the great storm in book 5 if Caesar had already conquered the elements in book 1.

Petronius does in fact provide a prose sea-storm, an excellent example of declamatory description.[2] The details are in the main Virgilian; the sea grows rough, the sails are reefed, the winds battle, the helmsman's art is ineffective. The sailor's prayer is followed by the crisis of the storm, a sudden gust and whirlpool, disintegration of the ship, death or rescue of the sailors. The only non-Virgilian feature is the fishermen, who put out *ad praedam rapiendam*. So in one of the Senecan declamations (*Contr.* 8. 6. 2) the rich man has his

---

[1] *Tr.* 1. 2; 1. 4; 1. 11. 19–24: literary storms at *Fast.* 3. 583–600; *Met.* 11. 474–569. See St. Denis, 345–56.

[2] *Sat.* 114: relevant also is the simile in *Sat.* 123 (*B.C.* 233–7), but it is in no way remarkable: its details (Virgilain in origin) are mostly found in Luc., 1. 498–504. For another (earlier) prose storm, see Curtius, 4. 3. 16.

eyrie above the sea—'illic iste naufragiorum reliquias computabat: illic vectigal infelix et quantum sibi iratum redderet mare'. In Seneca's *Agamemnon* Nauplius deliberately entices the fleet on to the rocks (557 sqq.); in Lucan the Nasamones are described (after the wreck of Cato's fleet on the Syrtes) as living off shipwrecks (9. 439-4 —sic cum toto commercia mundo / naufragiis Nasamones habent.

In the rhetorical schools descriptions of storms were *de rigeur*. 'Describe nunc tempestatem' says Cestius, and Seneca does not need to quote the description, for it was a stock passage (*Suas.* 3. 2: cf. *Suas.* 2. 8; *Contr.* 1. 4. 2). Two declaimers' descriptions may be quoted here, as showing the declamatory formula and its dependence on Virgil:

1. (*Contr.* 8. 6. 2): procul a conspectu reliqueram patriam . . . subito fluctibus inhorruit mare ac discordes in perniciem nostram flavere venti; demissa nox caelo est et tantum fulminibus dies redditus; inter caelum terramque dubii pependimus.
2. (*Contr.* 7. 1. 4): emicabant densis undique nubibus fulmina et terribili fragore horridae tempestates absconderant diem: imbres undique et omnia procellis saevientia . . . intumuerat subitis tempestatibus mare . . .

From these passages it can be seen where Lucan has kept to the declaimers' formula:

Contr. 8. 6. 2:	*Lucan, 5:*
procul . . . patriam	560. solvensque ratem dat carbasa ventis (cf. 576).
inhorruit mare . . .	564. niger inficit horror terga maris.
discordes . . . venti	566-7. flatusque incerta futuri turbida testantur conceptos aequora ventos.
	Amplified in 569-72; 598-612.
demissa nox caelo	627-8. non caeli nox illa fuit: latet obsitus aer infernae pallore domus nimbisque gravatus deprimitur.
tantum . . . redditus	630-1. lux etiam metuenda perit, nec fulgura currunt clara, sed obscurum nimbosus dissilit aer.
inter caelum . . . pependimus	638-42 (642). nubila tanguntur velis et terra carina.
	649. omni surgit ratis ardua vento.

There appear to have been three main contexts for the declaimers' descriptions. In *Contr.* 7. 1, the subject is the punishment of the parricide: this gives opportunity not only for descriptions of storms and other perils by sea, but also for *loci* on innocence, the declaimers ingeniously capitalizing on the antithesis between the security of the

innocent man and the raging elements outside. Cestius' hero is put
on a boat 'vix unius capax animae'; but his innocence brings divine
help—'ecce navis divinitus armatur'. The moral is drawn: 'magnum
praesidium in periculis innocentia. saevum mare volvitur, procellae
spumante impetu latera navigii urgent, pulsatur undique navis
periculis: innocentia tamen tuta est.'

Why then is Caesar saved in Lucan's storm? Such emphasis on
the episode must be intended to allude to the *parricida*, yet the guilty
man is saved. In contrast Pompey, who (for Lucan) certainly had
the greater claim to innocence, begins his last voyage in an inadequate
boat (8. 35–6):

> inde ratis trepidum ventis ac fluctibus impar
> flumineis vix tuta vadis evexit in altum.

It is Pompey's fear that Lucan emphasizes and the contrast between
Pompey the admiral, with a still appreciable fleet at Corcyra, and
Pompey the passenger (8. 37–9). In both passages the stormy sea is
symbolic of Fate—and Fate was on Caesar's side, as Pompey had
seen at the crisis on the field of Pharsalia (7. 647–8). But the parricide
was being saved for the death he deserved, which possibly was to
have been the climax of the completed poem.

The second context for declaimers' storm-descriptions is the third
Suasoria, where Agamemnon debates whether to sacrifice Iphigenia
or not. The *divisio* of this shows that the declaimers were concerned
with the question of how much trust to put in augury. Arellius
Fuscus, after describing changes of weather, led on to their causes
were they part of nature's regular disposition or was the moon
responsible? Mention of the moon opens the way for a description
of it and its appearance as a weather-sign, based on Virgil (*Georg.*
1. 427–37). A good storm-description should contain an account of
the portents, and for this Virgil's prognostics would be pressed into
service: Fuscus (*Suas.* 3. 4) dragged in his imitation willy-nilly—
'Vergilii versus voluit imitari; valde autem longe petit et paene
repugnantia materia, certe non desiderante, inseruit.' Lucan's storm
begins with 16 lines of prognostics (5. 541–56) of which five lines
concern the moon. The passages from Virgil, Fuscus and Lucan are
quoted here for comparison:

1. Virgil, *Georg.* 1. 427–35:

> luna revertentis cum primum colligit ignis,
> si nigrum obscuri comprenderit aera cornu,
> maximus agricolis pelagoque parabitur imber;
> at si virgineum suffuderit ore ruborem,   430

ventus erit: vento semper rubet aurea Phoebe.
sin ortu quarto (namque is certissimus auctor)
pura neque obtunsis per caelum cornibus ibit,
totus et ille dies et qui nascentur ab illo
exactum ad mensem pluvia ventisque carebunt . . .   435

2. Fuscus, Sen. *Suas.* 3. 4:
luna, quae sive plena lucis suae est splendensque pariter adsurgit in cornua,
imbres prohibet, sive occurrente nubilo sordidiorem ostendit orbem suum,
non ante finit quam lucem reddit, sive ne lunae quidem ista potentia est . . .

3. Lucan, 5. 546–50:
lunaque non gracili surrexit lucida cornu
aut orbis medii puros exesa recessus
nec duxit recto tenuata cacumina cornu
ventorumque notam rubuit; tum lurida pallens
ora tulit voltu sub nubem tristis ituro.

Aratus (*Phaen.* 778–818) is the origin of this: Virgil selected three main features—dullness of the moon as a sign of rain, redness as a sign of wind, brightness as a sign of fair weather. Fuscus, as Seneca unkindly pointed out, failed to improve on Virgil: 'Vergilius haec quanto simplicius et beatius dixit.' Lucan is only concerned with bad-weather signs (540): on the crescent horns, 546–7 imitates Virgil 433: 548 (a repetition of 546, not in Virgil) has its origins in Aratus (788–92: cf. Theophrastus, *Weather-signs* 27 and 38). On the redness, 549 imitates Virgil 430: Lucan's pale, cloudy moon (549–50) is fairly close to Virgil 428 in conception, but he has personified the moon by using *tristis*, as if she cannot bear to veil her beauty.[1]

The third context for declaimers' storms is provided by the first *Suasoria*, when Alexander debates whether to sail upon Ocean: certain aspects of this subject have been discussed above, pp. 17–18. The *suasoria* gave the greatest opportunity to the moralizers, such as Fabianus (sect. 9), who attempted to dissuade Alexander from sailing because to do so would be to tempt Fortune: this is, of course, just what Lucan's Caesar is doing—he has already reached the limits of *felicitas* before setting out in the boat, yet he deliberately goes further.[2] The Alexander *suasoria* also gave scope for description of the sea and speculation on its nature: storms had their place here—

[1] Note the symmetry of 550: *ora* at beginning balanced by *-uro* at end; three *t* sounds after *ora* matched by three *t* sounds before *-uro*; in middle of line, two *-ub* sounds, long and sad (cf. Virgil's *or* sounds in *Georg.* 1. 430). Nigidius, *De Ventis* 4 (= fr. cv, Swoboda), may have given Lucan material: so also Varro, as quoted by Pliny, *N.H.* 18. 349.
[2] There was in fact a *suasoria* in which Caesar deliberated whether to invade Britain or not (Quint. 7. 4, 2): Caesar's Fortune would certainly have figured in it.

D

Cestius said *Oceanus fremit*, and there is no knowing what hyperboles Musa (sect. 13) would have introduced.[1]

Finally, mention should be made of Seneca's storm (*Ag.* 465–578), the most rhetorical of all.[2] Whatever the extent to which Lucan drew on Seneca, it is most profitable to observe that both authors are writing in the same tradition and that they owe their similarities, not so much to direct imitation, as to a sharing of a common literary training.

[1] '. . . ut ignoscam Musae, qui dixit ipsis Charybdi et Scylla maius portentum: *Charybdis ipsius maris naufragium*, et, ne in una re semel insaniret: *quid ibi potest esse salvi, ubi ipsum mare perit?*

[2] See St. Denis, 405–6, 419–20. For later declaimers' storms see ps.-Quint., *Decl. Mai.* 6.5; 9.4; 12.16.

CHAPTER IV

LUCAN'S STORMS: ANALYSIS AND DISCUSSION

IN the previous chapter an attempt has been made to set Lucan's storm-writing in the context of the Roman literary and rhetorical tradition: we may now go on to examine the storm-passages in detail with a somewhat clearer idea of the relationship of Lucan's writing to that of his predecessors and contemporaries. First the four set-piece storms will be analysed.

I. 5. 504–677: CAESAR'S STORM

This is the most elaborate of the storms and closest to the traditional literary storm. Whether Caesar in fact ever took part in the rash adventure of the little boat is doubtful: he himself does not mention it (in *B.C.* 3. 18–30), but Valerius includes the episode under the heading *de temeritate* (9. 8. 2: cf. Luc., 5. 682) and in all probability found it originally in Livy. Suetonius (*D. J.* 58) and Plutarch (*Caes.* 38; cf. Appian, *B.C.* 2. 57–8) also mention it. Whether the episode was historical or not is for Lucan beside the point: the storm is symbolic, as other epic storms are—for example Aeneas' storm in book I of the *Aeneid* or the storm through which Polyneices goes in book I of Statius' *Thebaid*.[1] In Valerius, Caesar gave up his attempt to cross the Adriatic, yielding to necessity: no such attitude is to be found in Lucan's Caesar—his safe return to land is another example of Fortune's protection of her favourite, just as the voyage through the storm was the proving of Caesar's confidence in *his* Fortune. The storm is symbolic of Caesar's own tempestuous spirit, of Fortune's fluctuations, of the upheaval in the Roman world: through it all, Caesar is master—contrast his attitude to Fortune with that of Pompey later in the same book (5. 754–9), who sends Cornelia to hide in Lesbos where she will be safer than any tyrant (*tutior omni rege late*) and will provide a refuge for Pompey should Fortune turn against him. Nor is this the only contrast in the book: earlier the craven Appius had consulted the Delphic oracle (note too how the spiritual storm endured by the Pythia is symbolized by the volcano-simile at 5. 97–101), in strong contrast to the next episode

---

[1] *Theb.* 1. 336–89: see W-H. Friedrich, *op. cit.* (ch. 3, n. 3), 85–7.

(5. 237-373) in which Caesar confidently quells a mutiny. In the mutiny, as in the storm, Caesar rejoices to live dangerously and prove his good Fortune:

> fata sed in praeceps solitus demittere Caesar
> Fortunamque suam per summa pericula gaudens
> exercere venit; nec dum desaeviat ira
> exspectat; medios properat temptare furores (5. 301-4).

The storm may be divided into six parts:

I. *The prelude*, 504-59

Caesar leaves the camp at the third hour of the night and finds a boat moored in a cove. He is alone, save for Fortuna: Lucan lays emphasis on the contrast between Caesar's destiny and that of humbler beings (505-6; 509; 532-7). He finds the hovel of Amyclas, owner of the boat: in demanding to be ferried over to Italy he appeals to Amyclas' ambitions and desire for wealth. There is also an opportunity for Lucan to slip in a *locus communis* on the virtues of the simple life (527-31)—the other side of the coin, the palaces of the wealthy, comes elsewhere in the poem (10. 111 sqq.). Caesar himself, disguised as he may be in the clothing of a common man, betrays his rank by the arrogance of his speech.[1]

Amyclas, before reluctantly acquiescing in Caesar's demand (557-9), gives his storm-prognostics (540-56): the passage is based on Virgil (*Georg.* 1. 351-514), and goes back to Aratus and Theophrastus. The prognostics are divided into celestial and terrestrial: first comes the sun (541-5), whose setting without red clouds portended a storm, as did the assymetry of its setting rays and its disk, paler at the centre than at the rim.[2] Next follows the moon, for which five signs are given (546-50)—the crescent has 'blunted' horns and its central portion is not clearly defined; its extremities are neither tapering nor turned up (548: this hardly differs from line 546); it is red in colour, and its light, soon to be obscured by clouds, is dim.[3] For the terrestrial signs (551-6), six have been selected, two from nature and four

---

[1] Other authors (e.g. Val. Max., 9. 8. 2) give Caesar a slave's disguise; Lucan, in *plebeio amictu*, may intend allusion to the *tribunicia potestas* which identified the Princeps with the rights of the common people. Caesar, however much he was seen with the tribunes in public, was still *indocilis privata loqui*. For parallels in the passage, 504-39, see Virgil, *Aen.* 5. 22-3, 709-10 (Luc. 5. 510): Ovid, *Met.* 8. 630 (Luc. 5. 517) and 641-3 (Luc. 5. 524).

[2] For the sun cf. Virg., *Georg.* 1. 438-65 (which leads on to presages of war and disaster, including the Battle of Pharsalia): Sen., *Ag.* 460-4: Pliny, *N.H.* 18. 342-6: Aratus, *Phaen.* 819-89: Theophrastus, *W-S.* 27 Nigidius, fr. cvi (Swoboda).

[3] Cf. above, pp. 35-6: the original for the moon is at Virg., *Georg.* 1. 427-37: Arat. 778-818. Lucan 5. 559-60 does not appear in Virgil: but see Theophr. 27: Varro, quoted by Pliny, *N.H.* 18. 348-9, and cf. Sen., *Med.* 790· Nigidius, fr. cv (Swoboda).

from animals. All portend wind. They are: the movement of the trees; the beating of the waves upon the shore; the dolphin; the *mergus* (possibly a cormorant—cf. Ovid, *Met.* 11. 794) making for land; the heron in flight; the crow upon the shore, dipping its head in the waves.[1] All these signs are consistent with Lucan's setting— the Adriatic at night in the early spring: other signs will be given at the start of the storm itself (e.g. 561–4). Lucan had to be selective (for the material in Virgil was plentiful), the more so if, as is not unlikely, he made use of Varro, Aratus and his translators, even of Theophrastus.

II. *The storm rises,* 560–76

As Caesar and Amyclas set out the constellations are shaken by the winds. In Lucan, 1. 527–9, shooting-stars and comets are portents of war (as they were to Cicero, *de Div.* 1. 18); here they signify a storm.[2] Lucan believes that the winds cause the movement of comets and shooting-stars: he simplifies the connection between wind and comets, for he is not concerned with the scientific niceties of causation. This is as well, for the ancient philosophers differed widely in their explanations of the phenomena of comets: Lucan avoids discussion and instead employs hyperbole—even the fixed stars were moved by the winds. This is not as ridiculous as it at first seems, for the *fixa astra* are almost certainly comets that appear fixed: Aristotle, Seneca and Pliny had all distinguished between fixed and moving comets, and Lucan's remarks are in accordance with their theory.[3]

The tumult in the heavens is balanced by the threatening blackness and swelling of the sea.[4] Amyclas speaks again (568–76)—he advises giving up the voyage, for sea and sky together portend violent and unfavourable winds (the confused portents of the winds foreshadow the battle of the winds that is to come at 597–614): Corus (the north-west wind) will blow and against it no one can hope to reach Italy.

[1] See Virg., *Georg.* 1. 356–92; Pliny, *N.H.* 18. 359–65: cf. Arat. 909 sqq.: Theophr. 28–30, 38–42, 46–9. The ancient authors differ considerably on details of these prognostics.
[2] See Virg., *Georg.* 1. 365–7: Sen., *N.Q.* 1. 1. 11: Pliny, *N.H.* 2. 100, and cf. Arat. 926–32; Theophr. 13. Comets are discussed by Aristotle, *Met.* 1. 6–7 (344 b 19 sqq. for them as signs of wind); *Sen., N.Q.* 7 (esp. 6–8 and 28): Pliny, *N.H.* 2. 89–101—with which see Beaujeu's commentary (Budé ed. of Pliny, book 2, Paris 1950), 175–84.
[3] Arist., *Met.* 1. 7 (344 a 24): Sen., *N.Q.* 7. 6. 1 (from Epigenes); Pliny, *N.H.* 2. 91. For parallels in Luc. 5. 561–4, cf. Lucr. 2. 206–9: Virg., *Georg.* 1. 365–7; *Aen.* 2. 697.
[4] The tradition of the black swelling of the sea is: Hom., *Il.* 7. 64; 14. 16–19: Pacuvius, fr. 355(Warmington): Virg., *Aen.* 3. 195: Ovid, *Met.* 11. 480: Sen., *Ag.* 468–9. For the speech of Amyclas, cf. Palinurus at *Aen.* 5. 13–25 (esp. 22).

III. *Caesar's first speech*, 577–93

The second speech of Amyclas serves different purposes: it contrasts the timidity of the fisherman with Caesar's confidence and arrogance; it brings to an end the introductory part of the storm and its portents; it leads into Caesar's declaration of his identity and announcement of his high destiny—

> '. . . quaerit pelagi caelique tumultu
> quod praestet Fortuna mihi.'

He sees himself as the equal of the gods ('Italiam si caelo auctore recusas / me pete') and under the sure protection of Fortune. The structure of the episode is based on *Aen.* 1. 94–105; the arrogance of Caesar has something in common with the boasting of Ajax (cf. Sen., *Ag.* 545–52): the speech clearly sets forth the inner meaning of man against hostile nature, but a man who will triumph because of his Fortune, not, as will be the case with Cato in book 9, through his Virtue. Caesar's words are cut short, like those of Aeneas (*Aen.* 1. 102–5), by a sudden whirlwind which tears away the sails and seriously weakens the boat:[1] this feature of the literary storm is the prelude to the climax.

IV. *The climax of the storm*, 597–653

In outline this is the traditional literary storm:[2] it may be divided as follows:

1. 597–620. The winds, their battle and its effect on the sea
2. 620–24. Interlude: simile of Jupiter and the Flood.
3. 625–31. The air: clouds, rain, unnatural darkness.
4. 632–7. The heavens: thunder and shaking of the heavens.
5. 638–53. The ship: helplessness of the helmsman.

1. The battle of the winds (597–620)

This is the most detailed part of the storm: as Seneca (*Contr.* 8. 6. 2: see above, p. 34) shows, the battle of the winds was a standard exercise of the declaimer. Of the literary storms, Lucan here appears to have most in common with Seneca's *Agamemnon*.[3] The

---

[1] 593–6: besides Virgil, cf. Hom., *Od.* 5. 291 sqq.; 12. 403 sqq.: Pacuvius, fr. 363–5. For *turbo rapax* cf. Lucr. 1. 294: 'rapideque rotanti turbine portant', where the words catch the sound and motion magnificently in comparison to Lucan's alliteration of *p* and *t*.

[2] Cf. above, p. 34. For 'traditional' literary storms see especially Virg., *Aen.* 1. 102–22: Ovid, *Met.* 11. 484–543: Sen., *Ag.* 474–511.

[3] See St. Denis 419–20 for details: the battle of the winds is at Sen., *Ag.* 474–90 (for Luc. 5. 598 cf. also Sen., *H.F.* 594). Cf. Virg., *Aen.* 1. 81–6; 2. 415–9: Ovid, *Met.* 1. 61–6 (quoted by Sen., *N.Q.* 5. 16. 1) and 11. 490–1.

winds were the subject of philosophical speculation, and much ingenuity was exercised in naming them and assigning them to their correct place in the heavens.[1] Pliny (*N.H.* 2. 119) gives a brief resumé: the basic system was Homer's (*Od.* 5. 295–6), who makes Eurus, Notus, Zephyrus and Boreas to blow. By Aristotle's time there were eight literary winds; he increased the number to ten (with one extra local one, Phoenicias: *Met.* 2. 6) and Timosthenes made the number twelve. Pliny returns to the octagonal system, while mentioning the others. Seneca gives four main winds (*N.Q.* 5. 16. 1) and quotes Ovid (*Met.* 1. 61–6) and Virgil (*Aen.* 1. 85–6) for their names: as he points out, Virgil makes them all blow at once, which is an impossibility. He then gives Varro's dodecagonal system: just as Virgil had introduced the Greek literary winds to Latin epic, so (it would seem) Varro had been the intermediary for scientific discussion of them.

At any rate, Lucan takes four—Corus, Boreas (Aquilo), Eurus, Notus: he avoids Virgil's mistake—the sceptical *crediderim* at 610 implies that the last two are introduced merely for literary effect, to make his battle of the winds complete. He only vouches for the actual strife of Corus and Boreas: this was scientifically orthodox, for Aristotle had said that, while opposite winds could not blow at the same time, there was nothing to stop two that were not opposites (*Met.* 364 a 27). Lucan therefore takes two that would oppose a voyage from Greece to Italy: in giving Corus pride of place he follows Seneca, who alone distinguished between it and Argestes (generally taken as its Greek equivalent); for Seneca, Argestes was gentle, but Corus violent—'Cori violenta vis est et in unam partem rapax' (Sen., *N.Q.* 5. 16, 5: cf. Pliny, *N.H.* 2. 126 and 18. 338–9).

The hyperbole at 612–14 is remarkable. Ovid (*Met.* 1. 61–6) and Seneca (*Ag.* 479–84) had identified the winds by geographical references—*Nabataea regna* for Eurus, *Oceanus* for Corus, Scythia and the Strymon for Aquilo/Boreas, the Syrtes for Auster/Notus. Lucan improves on this by ingeniously supposing that each wind blew its local sea with it; thus the sea as a whole remained constant, while the actual water filling each basin had been changed.[2] The Adriatic, scene of the storm, was filled with the waves from the

---

[1] See Arist., *Met.* 2. 4–6: Sen., *N.Q.* 5: Pliny, *N.H.* 2. 114–34. Beaujeu's commentary (*op. cit.*, above, n. 6), 195–201 with the diagrams at the end of the book, is very helpful. The list of authors who speculated on the winds (Beaujeu, p. 195, n. 4) is impressive.

[2] See Housman's notes for this interpretation of *pelagus* (612) with the reading *priva* (for *parva*).

home of Corus, the Atlantic Ocean (617–20). The idea of the migration of the seas has its origin in the Stoic cataclysm: thus Seneca says (*N.Q.* 3. 29. 7–8):

> nihil erunt Hadriatici, nihil Siculi aequoris fauces, nihil Charybdis, nihil Scylla. omnes novum mare fabulas obruet, et hic qui terras cingit Oceanus extremas veniet in medium . . . peribit omne discrimen.

Similar to the present passage in Lucan is the migration of rivers in book 4 (116–17).

2. The simile of the Flood (620–4)

The battle of the winds and the other features of the storm are linked by this simile, which provides relief and stability at the height of the storm. The mention of the waves of Ocean (617 sqq.) has, as it were, lifted the storm out of its local context and given it universal aspect.[1] A simile, then, of the great Flood and the introduction of the gods is not out of place. Lucan was inspired by floods; there are five others in the poem,[2] evidence of the influence upon him of the Stoic doctrine of the cataclysm. Here Lucan makes Jupiter appeal to Neptune (Ovid, *Met.* 1. 274–5, had done the same). The alliance of wind (sky god) and wave (sea god) leads to the vast swelling of the sea: the next section follows on naturally.

3. The air (625–31)

Another hyperbole transfers the interest of the storm to the air and the thick clouds, which alone prevent the sea from reaching the stars. So thick are they that the darkness is not the darkness of the earth, but of the Underworld. Even this darkness cannot be lit by the *lux metuenda* of lightning which can scarcely force its way through the clouds. So closely do they compress the sea that the rain cannot fall: sea and rain are mingled in them.[3] Clouds, lightning, rain, darkness—all are features of the literary storm (cf. Ovid, *Met.* 11. 516–23 and 552; Seneca, *Ag.* 470–4). The Stoic doctrine on clouds is expressed by Seneca's *spissitudo aeris crassi* (*N.Q.* 2. 30. 4: cf. Virg., *Aen.* 5. 20): they are formed by water-vapour (so Aristotle,

---

[1] Thus at 639 it is sailors other than merely Caesar and Amyclas who are referred to—'si qui tum in mari erant' (Grotius).

[2] 1. 217–19 (Rubicon); 2. 209–18 (Tiber); 2. 408–10 (Po; cf. 4. 134); 4. 62–120 (Sicoris); 10. 215–18 (Nile).

[3] Duff (Loeb) misleadingly translates 629 by 'in the midst of the clouds the rain poured into the sea'—the word 'poured' destroys the point of the hyperbole. In 630 *lux metuenda* should refer to lightning, thus giving the proper weight to *metuenda*: so dreadful is the *pallor* that even lightning, normally a cause of terror, would be a comfort.

Met. 1. 9: 346 b 33), and Lucan's clouds are made all the thicker by the force of the wind condensing the vapour. Lucan deals more fully with lightning elsewhere (1. 151–7): Stoic theory held that it was caused by the collision of clouds.[1] Here Lucan's clouds were so thick that the lightning could only force its way through in feeble flashes (cf. Luc., 4. 76–8). In fact this phenomenon occurs in violent electric storms, where small flashes occur with hardly a pause.

Thus ends the description of the disturbance of the lower air.

4. The shaking of the heavens (632–7)

The collision of the clouds produces thunder as well as lightning, so violent that even the heavens quake at it. The lower air was the region of storms; a storm that could shake the celestial regions was a storm indeed (cf. Luc. 2. 267–71). Yet the hyperbole has its logic: thunder in the clouds corresponds to an earthquake on earth (Pliny, *N.H.* 2. 192), and earthquakes were caused, said the Stoics, by wind (Sen., *N.Q.* 6. 12. 1–2; cf. Arist., *Met.* 2. 8: 366 a 4): why should not the wind cause a sky-quake by its violence? And so the whole framework of the world and the harmony of Nature are threatened. If we supply *deis* with *spes una* in 636 (rather than *nautis*: cf. Sen., *Ag.* 485–7), the hyperbole is rounded off extravagantly—even the gods, normally having nothing to do with the disasters of mankind, are involved.[2]

5. The ship and sailors (638–53).

The celestial phenomena are ended and the description now returns to Caesar and Amyclas, although in lines 639 and 652 Lucan seems to be thinking of sailors in general. The details belong to the literary storm—the tossing of the boat from the depths to the heights, the helplessness of the helmsman, the opposing seas keeping the boat stable (cf. Homer, *Od.* 12. 413).[3] There is a succession of hyperboles: yet one should remember, before dismissing Lucan as extravagant, that even Virgil had said *rorantia vidimus astra* (*Aen.* 3. 567). The origin of the hyperbole at 649—*omni surgit ratis ardua vento*—is to be found in the Stoic theory of the cyclone which, says Seneca (*N.Q.* 5. 13. 3), can lift ships out of the water. This leads on

[1] Diels, *Doxographi*, p. 369: explained in Sen., *N.Q.* 1. 1. 6; 1. 14. 5; 2. 23. 1: cf. Pliny, *N.H.* 2. 135–6; Lucr. 6. 96 sqq. and 295 sqq.; Ovid, *Met.* 1. 56; 6. 695–6; 11. 435–6. The origin appears to be at Arist., *Met.* 2. 9.

[2] Cf. Sen., *Cons. ad Marc.* 26. 5. Parallels for Luc. 5. 632–7 may be found in Seneca at *Ag.* 485–7; *Thy.* 830–35; *H.O.* 1110–15. Cf. also Ovid, *Met.* 2. 299; Virg., *Aen.* 2. 354.

[3] For other details cf. Virgil, *Aen.* 1. 106–7; 3. 564–7: Ovid, *Met.* 11. 492–506: Sen., *Ag.* 507–9.

to the final hyperbole: it is not the islands between Italy and Epirus (e.g. Sason) nor the stormy shores of Greece (Thessaly seems to be misplaced here), but the summit of the Ceraunian mountains themselves that threaten shipwreck. Sason and Ceraunia are elsewhere connected by Lucan in reference to an Adriatic storm (2. 625–7): the promontory of Ceraunia was proverbially dangerous (e.g. Horace, Od. 1. 3. 20: Ovid, Rem. Am. 739), and Lucan intensifies the horror by wrecking his ship not on the rocks at its base but on the summit itself.

V. *Caesar's second speech, 653–71*

Caesar's first speech had heralded the climax of the storm: his second brings the description to an end, and all that remains thereafter is to bring Caesar to land and calm the seas. The former speech had challenged the fury of the sea and sky: the present one acknowledges the dangers he has provoked, worthy indeed of his great destiny (653–4). If he is now to die, he will die fearlessly, conscious that he has carried all before him abroad and at Rome (656–63): only the monarchy has eluded him (665–8). Other storm-tossed sailors feared death at sea and envied those who died on land and were sure of burial: Caesar needs no such honourable treatment: his spirit is greater than his body—let the latter be mutilated by the sea so long as the former lives to terrorize men everywhere (668–71). This utterance is worthy of the context: by it Lucan once again makes clear the symbolism of the storm and brings Caesar before us as something superhuman, to whom gods and men alike are insignificant opponents.

VI. *Caesar reaches land, 672–7*

Ajax had boasted and was destroyed: Caesar is saved, hurled on shore by a miraculous 'tenth wave'.[1] It remains for his followers to remonstrate (678–99), until dawn comes and the sea is calmed (700–2).

2. 3. 38–120: THE SPANISH FLOODS

This catastrophe is described by Caesar (B.C. 1. 48–52); it is not mentioned in the Livy epitome. Lucan's description, while owing much to Ovid's Flood (Met. 1. 262–347), derives its colour and some of the details from Stoic ideas of the Cataclysm.

---

[1] Cf. Hom., Od. 5. 313–440; Ovid, Met. 11. 530; Tr. 1. 49–50. See Paulus, ex Fest., s.v. *decumana* (p. 62, L), for 'size 10' eggs and waves.

I. *Prelude to the rainstorm* (48–75):

The hard, dry Spanish winter ends at the vernal equinox, and at the new moon (60) the East wind begins to dominate. It sweeps all the clouds before it until they are piled up over Spain, at the western limit of the world. The South wind was usually associated with rain and cloud; but Lucan's plan is better suited if the East wind is the bringer of rain, for it can drive the clouds before it from all the Eastern world. When they reach the furthest point of the world, where Ocean and the vault of heaven meet (cf. Luc., 7. 1–3), they pile up and the pent-up moisture bursts out. The idea of the wind sweeping the clouds of its domain before it has some similarity with the transference of rivers (4. 116–7) and the migration of seas (5. 612–14): Seneca (*N.Q.* 5. 18. 2) gives the Stoic doctrine on the subject.[1]

II. *Rain and floods* (76–109):

Caesar (*B.C.* 1. 48) agrees with Lucan that the floods were quite exceptional. At Lucan 76–8 the clouds are pressed tight against the vault of heaven and are forced to shed their load of moisture: there are similarities with 5. 627–31. Then the rainbow is introduced (79–82), 'drinking up' the sea and returning to the sky the moisture the clouds had shed.[2] Next the Pyrenean snows melt,[3] as in Caesar (*B.C.* 1. 48), and the way is open for the description of the floods (85–105).

The description falls into two parts, separated by a short exclamation against avarice (96–7). The first part elaborates Caesar's account, the second Ovid's: Seneca's cataclysm pervades the whole and supplies many details. Caesar's camp, placed between the rivers Sicoris and Cinga (thirty miles apart), was isolated and his foragers hemmed in: the result was a failure in the food supply and a steep rise in the price of grain. The context demands an attack on avarice (contrast Caesar's studied detachment in *B.C.* 1. 52) in which the poet ingeniously makes the hoarder of grain himself hungry, such is his thraldom to the *lucri pallida tabes* (perhaps an echo here of Persius, 4. 47). The description moves away from the camp and army at 98

---

[1] For 63, cf. Ovid, *Met.* 1. 61–2: for *fuscator* (66), Ovid, *Met.* 5. 285–6.

[2] Plaut., *Curc.* 129: 'bibit arcus: hercle credo hodie pluet'; cf. Virg., *Georg.* 1. 380–1 for this piece of folk-lore. Discussions of the rainbow at Aristotle, *Met.* 3. 2–5; Sen., *N.Q.* 1. 3–8: Pliny, *N.H.* 2. 150–1. Other refs. at Lucr., 6. 523–5: Hor., *A.P.* 18: Tib., 1. 4. 44: Ovid, *Met.* 1. 270–1. Aristotle, *Met.* 371 b 26 and 375 b 16, gives the lie to Duff's translation 'with its broken arch' at 79: Lucan means that the rainbow is semicircular.

[3] Possibly an echo of Livy, 21. 35. 6 and 21. 36. 6.

to the landscape: here Lucan varies Ovid's flood-description, while avoiding Ovid's *pueriles ineptias*, as Seneca had called them (*N.Q.* 3. 27. 12–13)—a Stoic flood needed to be described with restraint: 'scies quid deceat', said Seneca, 'si cogitaveris orbem terrarum natare.' And so it is suitable at this point to consider in more detail the parallels between Seneca's cataclysm (*N.Q.* 3. 27) and Lucan's: Seneca references come first, with the section number of ch. 27:

Sen., sect. 4: primo immodici cadunt imbres et sine ullis solibus triste nubilo caelum est; nebulaque continua, et ex humido spissa caligo.
Luc. 76–7: iamque polo pressae largos densantur in imbres / spissataeque fluunt.
Luc. 103–4: nec Phoebum surgere sentit / nox subtexta polo.

Sen. 5: inde vitium satis et segetum . . . marcor
Luc. 90–1: non pabula mersi / ulla ferunt sulci.

Sen. 6: labant . . . tecta
Luc. 89: castra labant.

Sen. 6: congestae saeculis tabuerunt nives, devolutus torrens . . . saxa revolutis remissa compagibus rotat.
Luc. 83–5: iamque Pyrenaeae, quas numquam solvere Titan / evaluit, fluxere nives, fractoque madescunt / saxa gelu.

Sen. 7: abluit villas et intermixtos ovium greges devehit.
Luc. 100–1: tecta ferarum / detulit atque ipsas hausit.

Sen. 7: . . . ruinam an naufragium querantur incertos.
Luc. 87: naufraga campo (arma).

Sen. 8: flumina . . . vasta . . . alveos reliquerunt.
Luc. 86–7: . . . tam largas alveus omnis / a ripis accepit aquas.

Sen. 8: quid tu esse Rhodanum, quid putas Rhenum atque Danubium quum superfusi novas sibi fecere ripas . . .? quanta cum praecipitatione volvuntur ubi per campestria fluens Rhenus . . . latissime velut per angustum aquas implet?
Luc. 116–17: . . . hos campos Rhenus inundet
hos Rhodanus, vastos obliquent flumina fontes.

Sen. 9: ferens secum . . . rupes deiectas.
Luc. 100: absorpsit penitus rupes.

Sen. 9: in orbem redit ingentemque terrarum ambitum atque urbium uno vortice involvit.
Luc. 99: , condidit una palus vastaque voragine mersit.

Sen. 10: quod olim fuerat nubilum, nox est: et quidem horrida et terribilis intercursu luminis diri. crebra enim micant fulmina . . .
Luc. 77–8: nec servant lumina flammas / quamvis crebra micent.

Sen. 10:   (mare) tunc primum auctum fluminum accessu . . . iam promovet
                litus: non continetur suis finibus, sed prohibent exire torrentes,
                aguntque fluctus retro: pars tamen maior . . . restagnat, et agros in
                formam unius lacus redigit.
Luc. 102–3:   (palus) reppulit aestus / fortior Oceani (cf. Luc. 1. 76–7).
Luc. 89:   alto restagnant flumina vallo.
Luc. 99:   condidit una palus.

The floods have destroyed the distinction between night and day,
one season and another, land and water—'rerum discrimina miscet
deformis caeli facies'. The description then is appositely rounded off
by the simile of the Antarctic (106–9), based on Virgil's two passages
on the Arctic (*Georg.* 1. 247–8 and 3. 349–83). There is a certain
majesty in the simile—whether it is unbroken winter or the warm
and flooded spring, the regular pattern of man's life is ruined when
the weather refuses its benign changes.

III. *Peroration* (110–20):

This is in the form of a prayer, leading up to the climax of 120.
Jupiter and Neptune are addressed, each god asked to flood the earth
with water from his element: besides the waters of sky and sea, the
waters of the earth itself will swell the flood—the rivers, the snow
and standing waters. Thus Spain will vanish and civil war cannot
be fought there—Lucan speaks as if it were easier to make the earth
vanish than eradicate the scourge of civil war.

In this episode Lucan has taken a regular literary theme and varied
it with particular emphasis on the Stoic cataclysm. Throughout
runs the moral theme (the *color* of the episode if it is regarded as a
rhetorical exercise), that Man deserves by his impiety (i.e. civil war)
to be destroyed by a second Flood.

.   .   .   .   .

There are four other passages where the final cataclysm is described
or alluded to.[1] At 1. 72–80 the collapse of Rome's greatness is
compared to the disintegration of the world and the final conflagra-
tion and cataclysm.[2] The collapse of Rome is again referred to in
cataclysmic terms at 2. 289–92: in such a disaster not even Cato can
remain impartial (2. 295). Again, at 7. 134–8, the issue of Pharsalia
is made universal: the signal for battle has been given, the day of
Rome's destiny has come. Portents of the end of the world are
seen, and Lucan expresses them in terms of the Stoic cataclysm

---

[1] See the appendix to chapter 4 (page 58) nos. 17–20 for the text of these passages.
[2] A difficult passage; see R. J. Getty's edn., notes *ad loc.* and App. B, 141–3.

accompanied by confusion of the elements.[1] Finally, there is the simile at 5. 620–4 (already referred to at p. 42 above).

·   ·   ·   ·   ·

3. 9. 319–47: The Storm off the Syrtes

The Syrtes were proverbial as a danger to mariners and Lucan introduces this episode with an account of them and their origin: like the Libyan serpents, their dangers seem to have been part of the Roman mythology of Africa.[2]

I. *The south wind lays the shoals bare* (319–23):

The storm begins in the traditional manner: as soon as the fleet reaches the high seas a 'black' wind arises (cf. Virgil, *Aen.* 1. 34–5 and 5. 8–11). The South wind, traditionally at home in the Syrtes, is pictured as defending its domain, blowing the water away from the sandbanks of the Syrtes. The situation derives from Apollonius (4. 1240–4), where the Argonauts are driven on shore by the tide, and from the wreck of Aeneas on the coast of Africa (*Aen.* 1. 106–112).

II. *Helplessness of the sailors* (324–9):

Lucan, not content with a vague reference such as Seneca's *ars cessit in malis* (*Ag.* 507), specifies the nautical techniques, as Livy had done (36. 44. 2). Either the sailors, in attempting to run before the storm, are caught by the sudden gusts, and their efforts to brail up the sails are frustrated by the wind, which wrenches the sheets and halyards from their hands so that the sails belly out beyond the ship, flapping uselessly: or, if the sailors had succeeded in brailing up the sails in time, sail, ropes and yard were all torn from the mast.[3]

III. *Wreck of part of the fleet and safe arrival of the rest* (330–47):

The ships which cut away their tackle were at the mercy of the tide: Lucan is more specific than Sallust[4] or Apollonius with *ventis*

---

[1] The passage can also be interpreted as a simile: the fear that men felt was similar to that which they would feel were the end of the world to come (*cernens*, 135, hypothetical). Other refs. to the violent end of the world in Lucan at 5. 181; 7. 812–15.

[2] Luc., 9. 308–18. Among the many refs. to the Syrtes may be mentioned Virg., *Aen.* 4. 41: Hor., *Od.* 1. 22. 5; 2. 6, 3; 2. 20. 15: Prop., 2. 9. 33: Tib., 3. 4. 9: Ovid, *Met.* 8. 120: Sall., *Jug.* 78. 2: Pliny, *N.H.* 5. 26. Lucan may have had some details from Strabo, 17. 3. 20; or Mela, 1. 7.

[3] 324–7 are difficult: *classibus* is understood as antecedent of *quarum*; by a bold hypallage it is the sheets and halyards that dare to deny the sails to the wind: *carbasa* is understood as subject of *vicere*. For the spondaic ending of 329 cf. Ovid, *Met.* 11. 456.

[4] *Jug.* 78. 2: 'nam duo sunt sinus . . . quorum proxuma terrae praealta sunt, cetera uti fors tulit alta alia, alia in tempestate vadosa. nam ubi mare magnum esse et saevire ventis coepit, limum harenamque et saxa ingentia fluctus trahunt.'

contraria volvens (333)—i.e. describing the current as sweeping in from the north. Perhaps here there is an intentional variant of the battle of the winds in the opposition of wind and current. These ships, then, were wrecked on the sandbanks: but those which were swept northwards by the wind reached the open sea and eventually came safely to shore at Lake Tritonis.[1]

.   .   .   .   .

4. 9. 445–92: THE LIBYAN DUST STORM

The uniqueness of this storm lies in the paradox at 455, *non imbriferam . . . nubem*. The storm is the first of the trials of Cato's *virtus* (cf. 444–5), and in this respect may be taken as symbolic of the adversity through which the *Romana iuventus* (481) must pass in the uphill road towards liberty and constitutional government (*durum iter ad leges*: 385). It has been discussed elsewhere; the following remarks, however, may be added.[2]

The storm is related to sea-storms (445–9): the perils of the Syrtes have been described, yet the storms that await the sailors on land are worse. At 449–71 the effects of the wind on the desert are described, with quasi-scientific explanations. The cave of the winds (468) finds a parallel in Seneca, *N.Q.* 5. 14. 1: the idea is connected with the Stoic doctrine of the earthquake. Just as in 5.632–3 the heavens were shaken by the winds, so here the winds, imprisoned in their cave, would shatter the framework of the world were it not for the fact that Libya, with its shifting sands, offers no solid resistance.[3] It is not surprising that details of Lucan's description of the dust storm belong to the repertory of the earthquake.[4] The description is embellished by two similes: the first (460–2) likens the raising of the dust to smoke rising from a fire and obscuring the sun; further point is added by *rapta*, for *rapere* is the key-word of the whole description.[5] The second simile (477–80), of the *ancilia*, serves to connect the description of the wind's effect with the reaction of Cato's men. In Lucan's other storms the similes have been taken from geography (4. 106–9) or mythology (5. 620–4): here Roman

---

[1] Parallels for Lucan's description of the episode at Ap. Rhod., 4. 1240–9 (Luc. 335–44): Virg., *Aen.* 1. 110–12 (Luc. 341–2) and 10. 303–4: Sen., *Ag.* 571–3 (Luc. 335–7).

[2] See M. Wünsch, *Lucaninterpretationen* (Leipzig, 1930), 50–8, who sees Livy as the source for historical elements in the episode, Posidonius (followed by Asclepiodotus, cf. Sen., *N.Q.* 6. 17. 4 and 2. 30. 1, and Seneca) for scientific elements.

[3] Cf. Sen., *N.Q.* 6. 23–4: Pliny, *N.H.* 2. 128.

[4] Cf. Luc. 459, 490, 492, with Sen., *N.Q.* 6. 22. 3 and 6. 25. 1.

[5] Cf. lines 455–7, 459, 465, 476, 479.

history is the source, as if the poet wished to remind the reader that Cato and his men were the true inheritors of the legacy of Roman tradition.

The climax of the storm is indicated by the paradox of 492, *qui nullas videre domos videre ruinas*. The point is more succinct than in the similar climax-passages of book 5 (636–7 and 650–3). Lucan's technique is to build up for the final *sententia* by several preparatory lines giving the background material: it is employed, for example, also at 4. 110–120 and 7. 514–520.

This completes the four extended storm passages. For contrast one may refer to the unusual description at 5. 424–55 of a storm that did not occur. The technique is familiar, with the onset of night and the departure from land; the description of air and sea (430–46), intensified by the triple geographical simile at 436–41 (cf. Virg., *Georg.* 3. 349 sqq.), and of the dangers and sufferings of the fleet and sailors (447–55). But all these features of the literary storm are employed when no storm occurs: the final point in this ingenious display is made by the paradox of 455—*naufragii spes omnis abit*.

We may now summarize the main elements of Lucan's storm-technique as follows:

1. Knowledge of the literary storm, with particular reliance on Virgil and Ovid.

2. Interest in philosophical speculation, especially on matters of meteorology and geography. This is largely Stoic in colour and includes Stoic doctrine on the final world flood and conflagration: there is much in common with Seneca, and the tradition appears to go back to Posidonius.

3. Interest in prognostics, derived largely from the *Aratea* and the first *Georgic*.

4. Knowledge of the sailor's art (Lucan is more exact than his predecessors).

5. Use of various literary devices:
   a. Pathos (sufferings of the victims of the storm, their hopes, prayers, fears).
   b. Intensification of horrors (especially by means of hyperbole and paradox).
   c. Simile (employed generally at a crisis in the storm, where a transition is needed).
   d. 'Pointed' lines (especially to close a passage), whose epigrammatic effect often relies on paradox.

  e. Verbal sound-effects (such as alliteration and assonance).[1]

6. Relevance of the storm to a wider theme (e.g. Caesar's *Fortuna*, Cato's *Virtus*). This may be emphasized by speeches from the characters involved or by declamatory passages (e.g. 4. 110–120) from the poet himself.

It remains now to draw attention to the similes and incidental passages where Lucan has used the vocabulary of the storm or related phenomena. It is difficult to make an exact classification: 20 similes, amounting to one-quarter of all Lucan's similes, are given here, of which 10 concern the sea, 4 storms on land or in the air, 4 the Cataclysm, and two the thunderbolt.[2]

The Marine Similes

(*a*) Two nautical similes:

  1. 6. 285–7: Torquatus withdrawing before Caesar's onset likened to a sailor reefing his sails. Perhaps the simile is taken from personal observation (*Circaeae* localizes the scene), but cf. Ovid, *Fast.* 3. 587.

  2. 9. 798–800: Nasidius, bitten by a *prester*, swells like a sail bellying before the north-west wind. A double simile, of which this, the nautical part, is unremarkable as description (except for the alliteration of *c*): the other part of the simile, the boiling water, derives from Virgil, *Aen.* 7. 462–6.

(*b*) Six similes of the stormy sea:

  3. 1. 498–504: the people deserting Rome in panic likened to sailors prematurely leaving their ship as a storm in the Syrtes hits them. One of Lucan's more extended similes, this is apposite and carefully worked out: the main features of the description (e.g. *turbidus Auster*; the collapse of the ship's mast) belong to the literary storm, but the diction and paradoxical conclusion are Lucan's own. The breaking of the mast is made more colourful by the sonorous *veliferi* (which does not, as one might expect, occur in Lucretius: see, however, Ovid, *Met.* 15. 719): the disintegration of the ship is hinted at by the harsh alliteration of *conpage carina*. The real point of the simile lies in 501 sqq.: the helmsman (Pompey) leaves his ship (Rome) before he need; and just as the crew bring upon them-

---

[1] Thus *s* for hissing of the wind at 5. 561–4: *t* for crashes at 4. 766–8; 5. 568; or the crunching of a boat on the beach at 5. 676–7; 9. 345–7; or heavy rain at 2. 502: *ur* for the roaring of the wind at 5. 549–50 and 566–8: *c* for the sharp cracking of a sail in the wind at 9. 799–800; or the breaking of a ship's planks at 1. 502: *f* for the strong wind at 2. 461; 6. 266.

[2] Cf. St. Denis, 421–5: Aymard, 91–2 and 99–100. The text of these passages is given in the appendix to this chapter, pp. 56–8.

E

selves the very thing they fear (*naufragium*), so the people flee into the very thing they are trying to avoid—*in bellum fugitur.*

4. 2. 454–61: the conflict of loyalty to Pompey and fear of Caesar in the minds of the Italians likened to the turmoil of the sea when the south and east winds blow. The battle of the winds and the cave of Aeolus are standard features of the literary storm: the compound adjectives vary the effect. The simile is not easy: Pompey is likened to the south wind (which hardly fits the part Lucan makes him play in 49 B.C.: he is static and passive in the similes at 1. 136 and 7. 125) and keeps his hold on the people of Italy, even although another force asserts his power elsewhere (the east wind over another element, the sky). But Fortune, now deserting Pompey and favouring Caesar, whose force is stronger than all else (the vigorous alliteration of *f* in 461 helps the point), sweeps away the loyalty of Pompey's supporters.

5. 3. 549–52: the disturbance of the water by the ships' oars likened to contrary motions of the sea when winds and tide are opposed. The reference here is to the opposition of current and wind (as at 9. 333–4), and the mention of two winds by name is merely formal: the surface of the sea (*fluctus*) moves with the wind, but the deep waters themselves (*mare*) obey the tide and current. The simile is carefully composed; note the symmetry of 551 and 552, the latter relying on quadruple chiasmus, anchored (so to speak) by the alliterative juxtaposition of the nouns in the central position. The balanced effect contrasts with the scene of confusion that is being described.

6. 6. 65–8: Pompey, unaware of Caesar's siege works, is likened to the inhabitant of inland Sicily or north Britain, ignorant of the tempest raging on the coast. A further point of the simile lies in the choice of islands—Caesar's fortifications encircle the Pompeian position as the sea does an island. The chief interest in the simile lies in the reference to Britain, reflecting the contemporary concern with the island (the revolt of Boudicca broke out in 61). It was a byword for stormy seas (cf. the lines of Albinovanus Pedo in Sen., *Suas.* 1. 15), and it was not until the governorship of Agricola (according to Tacitus *Agr.* 10) that the first Roman circumnavigation was made. Possibly Lucan's simile derives from a passage in Livy, book 105, in which Caesar's reconnaissance of Britain was described.

7. 6. 265–7: Pompey, in his efforts to break out of Caesar's blockade, likened to the sea battering at a cliff. The simile itself is undistinguished and the second part, the future collapse of the undermined

cliff, not very apposite. But it fulfils a useful function in effecting the transition from the Scaeva episode (with all its hyperbolical excitement) back to the main narrative. The sea, like A. H. Clough's 'silent . . . main', repulsed at one place, finds another where the defences of the land may be breached: so with Pompey as he probes Caesar's works—only there is an element of paradox in that in fact Pompey was the defender, Caesar the besieger. The subsequent simile of the Po (272–6) confirms the role of Pompey and the volcano-simile (293–5) adds to the effect. Not that all the power of nature is on one side: we have already seen that Caesar, too, has his share in a storm-simile at 286–7 (simile no. 1 above).

8. 7. 123–7: Pompey giving way to the demands of his army likened to the sailor allowing his boat to be blown about. The helplessness of the helmsman is, as we have seen, a feature of the literary storm. *Regimen*, used by Ovid (*Met.* 11. 552; cf. *ib.* 3. 593) and Petronius (*Sat.* 123–B.C. 235) in the concrete sense of the rudder, may be so used here by Lucan, although the abstract sense is equally applicable. Whether or not the simile has here passed over to metaphor, its real importance lies in the image of Pompey as helmsman: to the Republicans, from Cicero to Lucan, he was helmsman *manqué* of the ship of state, who failed to measure up to the task that faced him.

(c) Two similes of the sea after a storm:

9. 2. 187–90: the mutilated corpse of Marius Gratidianus likened to a man crushed by a fallen building or a corpse washed up from the sea. The obvious interest here lies in the first part with its reference, familiar from Juvenal's third Satire, to the dangers of life in imperial Rome. Yet, if we count those who perished *medio freto* among the victims of storms, we find that here too the motif of the storm is used to allude to the central theme of the Civil War. Certainly allusion is intended to the prophetic passage in book 1, where the frenzied matron cries (685–6):

> hunc ego, fluminea deformis truncus harena
> qui iacet, agnosco.

And the poet looks forward to the final scene in Pompey's tragedy, where his decapitated corpse, like Priam's (*Aen.* 2. 557–8), is rolled on the shore by the waves (8. 718–26).

. 10. 5. 217–18: the moaning of the Pythia after her frenzy likened to the sound of the sea after a storm. This feature usually finds its place in the literary storm as a prognostic (e.g. Luc., 5. 571–2): the simile is apposite, although the obvious parallel of the Pythia's spiritual turmoil with that of the sea is an overworked symbol in the fifth book, in view of what is to follow. The phrase *rauca gemit* is Virgilian (*Aen.* 9. 125, of a river).

Non-marine storm similes

11. 2. 267-71: the peace which Cato would enjoy, were he to stand aloof from the Civil War, likened to the peace of the upper air high above the storms of the air nearest the earth. This fine simile comes in Brutus' speech in which he attempts to dissuade Cato from taking sides in the war: it is fitting that the Stoic hero should be addressed in terms applicable to Stoic cosmology. The double simile is worked out exactly; the storm likened to war, the peace of the regions where the virtuous souls live likened to the inner peace of the virtuous man who abstains from an impious war. Thus Cato is identified with those good men whose souls belong to the upper regions—Lucan expounds this doctrine with the 'apotheosis' of Pompey at 9. 5-11. The simile appears in Seneca (*Ep.* 6. 7, 16): 'talis est sapientis animus qualis mundus super lunam: semper illic serenum est.' The doctrine of the lower air as the region of storms is stated by Seneca (*N.Q.* 2. 10-11) and Pliny (*N.H.* 2. 102-4): from Cicero (*N.D.* 2. 21. 56) it appears that the doctrine went back to Posidonius. Cicero specifically mentions *fortuna* and *temeritas* as being absent from the upper regions, *veritas* and *constantia* as being present: these are precisely the qualities that Lucan attributes respectively to Caesar and Cato.

In this simile, line 268 deserves attention, both for its symmetrical arrangement and for its use of the *s* sound, indicative of the smooth and silent progress of the planets. To the Virgilian *volvuntur sidera lapsu* (*Aen.* 4. 524) Lucan has added the notion of *inconcussa*, in allusion to the Stoic doctrine that stormy winds shook the stars and caused the flaming comets.[1]

12. 2. 501-2: the javelins hurled by Caesar's men likened to heavy rain. This simile is like no. 13: for part of its effect it depends on the harsh dentals, *t* and *d*, of 502.

13. 3. 482-4: missiles bounce off a *testudo* like hail on a roof.[2]

---

[1] This appears to be the meaning of *ventos tractusque coruscos flammarum* (269-70), rather than the insipid 'long flashes of flame' of the Loeb translation: cf. Lucr., 2. 206-9: Lucan, 5. 561-4 and above, p. 40.

[2] Cf. Aymard, 84-5: parallels in Ap. Rhod., 2. 1083: Virg., *Aen.* 5. 458: Ovid, *Met.* 12. 480: Sen., *Ep.* 45. 9.

14. 4. 766–8: the cloud of dust raised by Juba's cavalry likened to that raised by the north wind. The real point of the simile lies not so much in the dust-cloud as in the comparison of the cavalry to a storm-wind; this interpretation is borne out by the harsh alliteration (*t* 14 times in three lines). *Bistonius* is used to express the ferocity of the storm-wind, rather than its locality: in any case, a dust-cloud raised in Thrace would hardly deserve mention, compared with a genuine Libyan dust-storm (as at 9. 455–62).

Similes of the thunderbolt

15. 1. 151–7: Caesar likened to lightning. This fine simile is the high point in Lucan's introductory portrait of Caesar, balancing the static tree-simile (1. 136–143) used for Pompey. The simile has been discussed elsewhere:[1] it is worth drawing attention here to Quintilian's reference (in his discussion of hyperbole, 8. 6. 71) to a simile from a (lost) Hymn by Pindar in which Hercules is likened 'non igni nec ventis nec mari, sed fulmini . . . ut illa minora, hoc par esset'.

16. 3. 315–20: the Civil War compared to the Jupiter's fight against the giants. This simile is included with storm-passages because the theme of war in heaven is related to the battle of the elements or of the winds: it is used twice elsewhere by Lucan (1. 34–6; 7. 144–150). The crafty Greeks of Massilia here are pleading to be allowed to remain neutral in the war: they have no more right, say they, to take sides than mortals would in war among the immortals. The Romans are flatteringly identified with a superior order of beings: more insidiously, Caesar is identified with the king of the gods, whose supreme power is displayed by the thunderbolt —to which Caesar has already been likened. Nor would Lucan's readers fail to recall the opening lines of Horace's Ode to Augustus (3. 5)—'caelo tonantem credidimus Iovem regnare': the allusion to the tyranny that replaced the free Republic is overt—*praesens divus habebitur. . . .*

Similes from the Cataclysm

17–20. 1. 72–80, 2. 289–292, 5. 620–4, 7. 134–8. These have already been mentioned above, p. 47.

Finally there are three minor storm-references to be mentioned. At 1. 406–8 the harbour of Monaco is described indirectly by the reference to the local wind, whose violence is witnessed to by Pliny

---

[1] See Aymard, 99–100 and refs. in Getty's notes, *ad loc.* Alexander is *terrarum fatale malum fulmenque* at Luc., 10. 34.

(*N.H.* 2. 121): Augustus had dedicated a temple to it (Sen., *N.Q.* 5. 17. 4).

The two passages at 8. 35–9 and 9. 113–16 are complementary: in the first, Pompey leaves Greece in a tiny boat; in the second, Cornelia hides in the hold of her ship, unmoved by the storm outside. The connection of both passages with the declaimers' *locus* on innocence (cf. above, pp. 34–5) is clear: so also is the symbolism as the defeated Pompey leaves his former greatness and faces the storms of adversity armed only with his innocence; or as the grief-stricken Cornelia withdraws from the turbulent world to devote herself to her love for her dead husband.

This survey of Lucan's use of storms and the sea has shown how deeply these aspects of nature affected him. We have traced (in chapter III) the literary and rhetorical tradition and have seen that Lucan was well acquainted with it; moreover that he was influenced by the attitudes of his own contemporaries, both those whose concern was directly with trade and exploration and those philosophers whose speculations included meteorological phenomena. Yet these traditions and influences do not account for the whole of Lucan's treatment; for we find in addition an enthusiasm for and considerable knowledge of the sea and meteorology which, combined with the training of a declaimer, give Lucan's writing an interest often lacking in that of his successors or even some of his predecessors. His fault lies (conspicuously in the book 5 storm) in a mistaken sense of proportion; his intentions are clear, his execution skilful—yet the progress of the epic is obstructed by this very skilfulness. Nowhere is this aspect of Lucan more clearly to be seen than in his handling of divination and magic, to which we shall now turn.

APPENDIX

So as to spare the reader a lot of troublesome cross-referring to the text of Lucan, the similes and incidental references discussed on pages 51–6 are given here.

1. 6. 285–7: Torquatus ruit inde minax, qui Caesaris arma
   segnius haud vidit, quam malo nauta tremente
   omnia subducit Circaeae vela procellae.
2. 9. 798–800: spumeus accenso non sic exundat aeno
   undarum cumulus, nec tantos carbasa Coro
   curvavere sinus.
3. 1. 498–504: Qualis, cum turbidus Auster
   reppulit a Libycis inmensum Syrtibus aequor

fractaque veliferi sonuerunt pondera mali,
desilit in fluctus deserta puppe magister
navitaque, et nondum sparsa conpage carinae
naufragium sibi quisque facit; sic urbe relicta
in bellum fugitur.

4. 2. 454–61: . . . ut cum mare possidet Auster
flatibus horrisonis, hunc aequora tota secuntur:
si rursus tellus pulsu laxata tridentis
Aeolii tumidis inmittat fluctibus Eurum,
quamvis icta novo, ventum tenuere priorem
aequora, nubiferoque polus cum cesserit Euro,
vindicat unda Notum. facilis sed vertere mentes
terror erat, dubiamque fidem fortuna ferebat.

5. 3. 549–52: Ut, quotiens aestus Zephyris Eurisque repugnat,
huc abeunt fluctus, illo mare, sic ubi puppes
sulcato varios duxerunt gurgite tractus,
quod tulit illa ratis remis, haec rettulit aequor.

6. 6. 65–8: . . . veluti mediae qui tutus in arvis
Sicaniae rabidum nescit latrare Pelorum,
aut, vaga cum Tethys Rutupinaque litora fervent,
unda Caledonios fallit turbata Britannos.

7. 6. 6. 265–7: (nec magis . . .) quam mare lassatur, cum se tollentibus Euris
frangentem fluctus scopulum ferit aut latus alti
montis adest seramque sibi parat unda ruinam.

8. 7. 123–7:   . . . sic fatur et arma
permittit populis frenosque furentibus ira
laxat et ut victus violento navita Coro
dat regimen ventis ignavumque arte relicta
puppis onus trahitur.

9. 2. 187–190:   . . . sic mole ruinae
fracta sub ingenti miscentur pondere membra,
nec magis informes veniunt ad litora trunci,
qui medio periere freto.

10. 5. 217–18:   . . . ut tumidus Boreae post flamina pontus
rauca gemit, sic muta levant suspiria vatem.

11. 2. 267–71:   . . . sicut caelestia semper
inconcussa suo volvuntur sidera lapsu.
fulminibus propior terrae succenditur aer,
imaque telluris ventos tractusque coruscos
flammarum accipiunt: nubes excedit Olympus.

12. 2. 501–2:   . . . crebroque simillima nimbo
trans ripam validi torserunt tela lacerti.

13. 2. 482–4: dum fuit armorum series, ut grandine tecta
innocua percussa sonant, sic omnia tela
respuit.

14. 4. 766–8: tum campi tremuere sono, terraque soluta,
quantus Bistonio torquetur turbine, pulvis
aera nube sua texit traxitque tenebras.

15. 1. 151–7: qualiter expressum ventis per nubila fulmen
    aetheris inpulsi sonitu mundique fragore
    emicuit rupitque diem populosque paventes
    terruit obliqua praestringens lumina flamma;
    in sua templa furit, nullaque exire vetante
    materia magnamque cadens magnamque revertens
    dat stragem late sparsosque recolligit ignes.

16. 3. 315–320:   . . . si caelicolis furor arma dedisset,
    aut si terrigenae temptarent astra gigantes,
    nec tamen auderet pietas humana vel armis
    vel votis prodesse Iovi, sortisque deorum
    ignarum mortale genus per fulmina tantum
    sciret adhuc caelo solum regnare Tonantem.

17. 1. 72–80:   . . . sic, cum conpage soluta
    saecula tot mundi suprema coegerit hora,
    antiquum repetens iterum chaos, omnia mixtis
    sidera sideribus concurrent, ignea pontum
    astra petent, tellus extendere litora nolet
    excutietque fretum, fratri contraria Phoebe
    ibit et obliquum bigas agitare per orbem
    indignata diem poscet sibi, totaque discors
    machina divolsi turbabit foedera mundi.

18. 2. 289–92: sidera quis mundumque velit spectare cadentem
    expers ipse metus? quis, cum ruat arduus aether,
    terra labet mixto coeuntis pondere mundi,
    compressas tenuisse manus?

19. 5. 620–4:   . . . sic rector Olympi
    cuspide fraterna lassatum in saecula fulmen
    adiuvit, regnoque accessit terra secundo,
    cum mare convolvit gentes, cum litora Tethys
    noluit ulla pati caelo contenta teneri.

20. 7. 134–8:   . . . quis litora ponto
    obruta, quis summis cernens in montibus aequor
    aetheraque in terras deiecto sole cadentem,
    tot rerum finem, timeat sibi? non vacat ullos
    pro se ferre metus: urbi Magnoque timetur.

21. 1. 406–8:   . . . non Corus in illum
    ius habet aut Zephyrus, solus sua litora turbat
    Circius et tuta prohibet statione Monoeci.

22. 8. 35–9: inde ratis trepidum ventis ac fluctibus inpar,
    flumineis vix tuta vadis, evexit in altum.
    cuius adhuc remis quatitur Corcyra sinusque
    Leucadii, Cilicum dominus terraeque Liburnae
    exiguam vector pavidus correpsit in alnum.

23. 9. 113–16: illam non fluctus stridensque rudentibus Eurus
    movit et exsurgens ad summa pericula clamor,
    votaque sollicitis faciens contraria nautis
    conposita in mortem iacuit favitque procellis.

Chapter V

DIVINATION AND MAGIC

ANY classical epic worth the name had a storm: another standard feature, at any rate of Roman epic, was prophecy and (generally) superstitious ritual. This is hardly surprising if one considers the naturally superstitious character of the Romans, the enormous part that divination played in Roman public life, and the flood of speculation about matters supernatural that swept Rome under the Julio-Claudians in the wake of the collapse of the old official religion. The surprising fact is the virulence of the criticism of Lucan by modern scholars for giving so much space to these matters: his Erictho scene 'has little *raison d'être* save the gratification of the taste for witchcraft which Lucan shared with his audience' (Butler): Heitland finds that 'the witch of the hour takes up 63 lines of unspeakable foulness and horror'. The enthusiasm of Bourgéry may be excessive, but it leads to a more just estimate of what Lucan was trying to do.[1] There are three main passages which deal with divination and magic: in book 1. 522–695 prodigies at Rome are enumerated and are then interpreted by three seers—a professional *haruspex*, a learned astrologer, and a raving matron. In book 5. 67–236 there is a digression on the Delphic oracle; and in book 6. 413–830 there is the celebrated episode of the witch Erictho and her necromancy. To these should be added the few lines in book 9. 544–86, where Cato stands before the oracle of Jupiter Ammon and expounds the virtuous man's attitude to divination. One-tenth of the poem (as it stands) is a large proportion to devote to these subjects, especially in a poem which is self-consciously historical epic, in that it eschews the apparatus of divine intervention. One can only observe, while admitting that Lucan has been disproportionate in his treatment, that the episodes do fit into the plan of the

[1] A. Bourgéry, 'Lucain et la Magie', *R.E.L.* 6 (1928), 299 sqq. Other works helpful on the subject are: L. Fahz, *De Poetarum Romanorum Doctrina Magica* (Giessen, 1904: = Dietrich and Wünsch, *Relig. Versuche*, ii. 3): T. Hopfner, art. 'Mantike', *R-E* 14, col. 1258: C. Preisendanz, *Papyri Graecae Magicae* (Leipzig, 1928), esp. vol. 1, 64–180: F. Cumont, *Les Religions Orientales dans le Paganisme Romain* (Paris, 1929) and *After-life in Roman Paganism* (New Haven, 1923). Most recently (after the present chapter had been completed), B. F. Dick, 'The Technique of Prophecy in Lucan', *T.A.P.A.* 94 (1963), 37–49. In general, A. S. Pease's edition of Cicero, *De Divinatione* (*Univ. of Illinois Studies in Lang. and Lit.*, 6, 1920 and 8, 1923), has been very useful.

poem—and Lucan's aim, after all, was not to tell the story as briefly
and directly as possible. Each precedes a new chapter in the tragedy:
the book 1 episode sets the stage for Caesar's domination of Italy
and Pompey's departure; Appius' visit to the Delphic oracle intro-
duces a new stage in the war, when the West has been lost to
Pompey and all now turns on events in Greece and the East. It acts
as a bridge, so to speak, between the events in Italy, Gaul, Spain and
Africa, and the campaign in Greece that is to find its fatal climax on
the field of Pharsalia. Moreover, the fifth book is turbulent: the
spiritual turmoil of the Pythia is balanced by the physical turmoil of
the great storm—both symbolic of the great events that are about to
be played out. Again, in the sixth book, it is true that the Erictho
episode holds up the action of the poem when the reader is impatient
for affairs to move to the crisis: but the episode is necessary (if not
at such length) as a prelude to the disaster of Pharsalia in order to
prepare the reader for the full horror of coming events. In particu-
lar, the climax of the episode with its pageant of Roman dead, good
and evil, recalls, and contrasts with, the pageant at the end of the
sixth *Aeneid*: Virgil's epic was about the founding of the Roman
people, Lucan's about the destruction of their liberty.[1]

As for the inordinate length of the episodes, this is explained by
the care Lucan takes with subjects for which he has a genuine
enthusiasm—this has already been observed in the case of storms;
another example is the serpent episode in book 9. The three con-
spicuous features of his divination or magic passages are, firstly, a
minute knowledge of procedure and technical details; secondly, a
ruthlessly unsqueamish power of description; thirdly, speculation
about the meaning or validity of what is being described (as at
5. 86–99 or 6. 492–9). Whether these passages are unpleasant or not
is a matter of taste: they do not offend the canons of post-Virgilian
epic.

At 6. 425–30 Lucan gives a list of the various ways of inquiring
about the future. They are as follows: 1. Oracles (Delos, Delphi
and Dodona are named); 2. extispicy, augury and the art of the
haruspex; 3. astrology; 4. 'secret, but lawful, knowledge' (a vague
phrase covering anything that Lucan has no knowledge of). Finally,
there is 'unlawful knowledge'—in particular necromancy. This
classification amplifies Cicero's distinction between intuitive (or
natural) divination and inductive (or artificial) divination (Cic., *De*

---

[1] See A. Guillemin, '*L'Inspiration Virgilienne dans la Pharsale*', *R.E.L.* 29 (1951), 214–27.

Div. 2. 26): only the first of Lucan's group is 'natural', that is, direct inspiration by a god; the others are all 'artificial'. And Lucan succeeds in giving, in his three passages, examples of every one of his types of divination, with the exception of augury. In book one, the three seers represent haruspicy and extispicy (Arruns: his skill at augury is also mentioned at 1. 588 but is not exemplified); astrology (Nigidius); and direct inspiration (the *matrona*). In book 5, the Delphi episode is a full treatment of 'natural' divination; the book 6 passage deals with the black art of necromancy.

The book 1 passage is prefaced by 60 lines of portents (522–83), indicative of the grave crisis in Roman affairs and resulting in panic at Rome. Such lists appear in the sober pages of the historians (e.g. Livy, 3. 10. 6), who anyway often had little else in the way of source-material: Lucan, however, is here following Virgil (*Georg.* 1. 463–92), whose comparable list of portents concerned the death of Caesar. To a lesser extent he had Ovid (*Met.* 15. 779–802) and Tibullus (2. 5. 71–8) as his models. A similar portent-passage, prefacing a disaster, comes at 7. 151–80 (a passage which has affinities with Valerius Maximus, 1. 6. 12, and may therefore have been something of a rhetorical *locus*). The first section of the portents (526–44) is concerned with the sky, and is closed by the Thyestes simile: this is apposite indeed for a civil war where *cognatas acies* are involved and the right hand of the Roman people is turned against its own entrails (see Lucan 1. 2–4)—brother against brother, a people consuming their own flesh. Next follow volcanic and seismic prodigies; even in these, nature is thrown out of its regular ways —Etna's eruption has no upward force, the waves of Charybdis are bloody. Included in the prodigies of fire are the sacred fires of Rome, the Vestal hearth and the ritual fire at the closing of the Latin festival: in these two places the flame symbolizes the unity of the family and the unity of the wider family that is Rome, and its failure or division can only portend intestine war: again mythology is called in to exemplify fraternal strife. The rest of the passage (556–83) gives various portents experienced by the common people of Rome: within the city, prodigies among the temples and statues of the gods, appearances of wild beasts and monstrous births, dire prophecies magnified by popular rumour, frenzied utterances by the fanatic (if virile) followers of Bellona and the emasculated Galli, groans from the ashes of the dead. Outside were the sound of arms and loud cries, while the peasants fled before the apparition of a giant Fury, portending war and punishment, whose victims were driven mad—the madness of impious war and civil strife. Appropriately mythology can alone suffice to close the passage (it would seem), as reference is made to Agave, Lycurgus, Hercules—all blinded by divine wrath and so maddened as to wreak their own destruction or that of their kin. Yet this is not all: for Lucan mythology is too distant in time and place; the horror of the coming war can best be expressed at the climax of the episode (578-83) by evoking the ghosts of Marius and Sulla, leaders in the earlier war of Roman against Roman.

Such portents call for interpretation: the three seers whom the poet introduces are progressively clearer in their burden. First comes the Etruscan *haruspex*, Arruns (584-638). Cicero (*De Div.* 2. 11) tells us that it was the custom for Etruscan seers to be summoned in moments of national doubt, and Livy (1. 56) vouches for the antiquity of the custom. But in the late republic the *haruspices* had lost their ancient prestige: the father of the Gracchi called them 'barbarian' (Cic., *N.D.* 2. 11), while the elder Cato found them ridiculous (Cic., *De Div.* 2. 51). Cicero thought it a disgrace that in his day men were senators who had formerly been *haruspices* (*Ad Fam.* 6. 18. 1). But under Claudius there had been a revival: in A.D. 47 the pontifices were ordered by a SC to organize the college of *haruspices*, to prevent so ancient an institution from petering out (Tac., *Ann.* 11. 15): according to Tacitus it was public indifference and new and imported religions that had led to this state of affairs. In Lucan's lifetime, then, the Etruscan *haruspices* were in the public eye, and Lucan had some excuse for introducing an anachronism and for displaying his knowledge of the art of the Etruscans. Not that he, any more than his sophisticated and sceptical contemporaries, believed in Claudius' efforts at antiquarian revivalism; philosophy was preferable to archaic superstition.[1] It comes as no surprise that Arruns can mumble no more than a few dark hints of impending disaster, wrapped up in riddling circumlocutions (638).

First (down to 609) come the preparations for Arruns' sacrifice: there is a ritual destruction of *monstra*, followed by a lustration of the *pomoerium* attended by the pontifices, the lesser priestly colleges, the Vestals, the quindecimviri, the augurs, the septemviri, the Titii, Salii and flamens. While this procession goes on Arruns himself buries traces of fallen thunderbolts (cf. Luc., 6. 520; 8. 864). The lustration is a *tour de force*, for in these few lines Lucan introduces the complete personnel of the Roman state religion, sometimes with

[1] Cf. Luc., 9. 581-2: Sen., *N.Q.* 2. 32: Cic., *De Div.* 2. 52.

additional learned details. Then comes the sacrifice itself (609–29), a failure in the deed and in its sequel. In describing the ill-omened entrails Lucan had little scope for originality, for of the Greeks Sophocles and Euripides had written such descriptions, and were followed by Seneca, who certainly was Lucan's immediate model here.[1] Finally Arruns utters his *ambages* (631–8), dark, dire and deprecatory.[2]

Extispicy has failed; in place of the *haruspex* the astrologer is brought on (639–72). Nigidius was a historical figure, one of the two pillars of scholarship (the other was Varro) in the age of Caesar, according to Aulus Gellius (19. 14. 3), who also refers to the obscurity of his writings.[3] There were several reasons why Lucan should have some sympathy with him: his republicanism (for Nigidius supported Pompey in 49, was exiled by Caesar and died in exile);[4] his Neo-pythagorean philosophy;[5] his skill in astrology, a science which was extremely popular under the early Empire and likely to appeal to Lucan for its blending of exact observation with occult mumbo-jumbo. Indeed, the present passage is a display-piece, in which the poet shows off his knowledge of the dodecatrope—that what he says is almost completely inaccurate (as far as the position of the planets in January of 49 B.C. is concerned) does not greatly affect Lucan's purpose.[6] The real significance of the prophecy lies in its republicanism—the rest is persiflage.

The prophecy is more rhetorical than the utterance of Arruns, calmer (yet more obscure) than that of the matron. It opens with a statement of two views of destiny (641–4) of which the second, the Stoic doctrine, is implicitly accepted: Fate has a disaster in store, and

[1] Soph., *Ant.* 1005–11: Eur., *Elect.* 810–29: Sen., *Oed.* 303–83.

[2] For extispicy see Pease on Cic., *De Div.* 1. 16 (pp. 94–8). Varro (referred to by Schol. Dan. on *Aen.* 3. 359 and Isid., *Etym.* 8. 9. 13) was probably one of Lucan's sources; so may Claudius have been, who wrote a history of Etruria (Suet, *Claud.* 42). For Tages see Cic., *De Div.* 2. 50–1 (cf. Ovid, *Met.* 15. 558–9).

[3] For Nigidius see W. Kroll, art. 'Nigidius' (no. 2), *R-E.* 17, col. 200: *P. Nigidii Figuli Opera*, ed. A. Swoboda (Amsterdam, 1964); works which Lucan may have consulted would be N.'s *De Extis* (cf. Gellius, 16. 6. 12) and *Augurium Privatum* (id., 7. 6. 10). See also J. Carcopino, *La Basilique Pythagoricienne de la Porte Majeure* (Paris, 1926), 196–202: C. S. Floratos, Ἡ προφήτεια τοῦ *P. Nigidius Figulus* (Athens, 1958: cf. review by R. J. Getty in *J.R.S.* 51 (1961), 270). Cf. Cic., *Timaeus*, fr. 1.

[4] Jerome, *Chron.* a. Abr. 1972.

[5] See R. J. Getty, 'Neopythagoreanism in Lucan', *T.A.P.A.* 91 (1960), 310 sqq. for the suggestion that Lucan constructed the passage in accordance with Pythagorean ideal proportions: also Getty, 'The Astrology of P. Nigidius Figulus', *C.Q.* 35 (1941), 17 sqq.

[6] See Housman's edn., 325–7 and Getty, art. cit. (*C.Q.*), in previous note. For the popularity of astrology cf. the success of Ptolemy's *Tetrabiblos*, and see F. E. Robbins' intr. to his Loeb translation (London, 1948), ix–x. A good modern account is in Cumont's *Les Religions Orientales* (above, note 1), ch. 7. For the dodecatrope see Getty's articles already cited: Lucan probably used Manilius, *Astron.* 2 (esp. 856–967).

whatever it is (various natural disasters are mentioned as possibilities
in 645–50) one thing is certain, many men are to die on the same
day. A universal disaster is portended—nothing less than the final
cataclysm or conflagration: yet for these the planets are not in the
right position (651–8). It is war that threatens, for the benign
planets, Jupiter and Venus, are hidden and Mercury is still; Mars
possesses the sky (658–63).[1] It will be no ordinary war, for it will
destroy all the normal usages of civilized man (666–7), so that crime
will be called virtue: yet its end will be worse than itself, for the
sequel will be a tyranny and the end of Roman liberty.

Arruns has hinted at disaster: Nigidius has (for the first time in
the poem) warned of the coming tyranny: it is left now for the
matron to make it clear to the panic-stricken citizens what they
should now fear. The former seers, representatives of 'artificial'
divination, have spoken in dark generalities or scholarly dilemmas:
the matron, directly inspired by the god (678), carries conviction
by her intensity; she raves, yet is the most explicit of the three. The
stage is carefully set for her; she is heralded by a simile expressive of
the pent-up force of the god within her.[2] Her utterance is excited,
and Lucan maintains the impression by the short questions, dis-
jointed sentences, and by the use of the present tense (the others had
used the future).[3] She sees before her both the coming civil war and
its successor; Pharsalia, the murder of Pompey, Thapsus, Massilia,
Munda, the murder of Caesar, Philippi—all are brought before the
pavida plebs.[4] The matron is released by the god; she collapses ex-
hausted; the book ends and the prologue to the tragedy is complete.

The three seers in book 1 foreshadow more extended passages:
the artificial divination of Arruns is developed in the necromancy
of Erictho, where the contrast between the official ritual of the
haruspex and the activities of the witch is exploited. Nigidius'
astrology finds no further development, but his message—the kernel
of which is *cum domino pax ista venit* (670)—is fully worked out in
the story of Scaeva (6. 138–262), the type of perverted virtue,
recalling the words of Nigidius at 1. 667–8: *scelerique nefando nomen
erit virtus*: the cause in which Scaeva performs his heroic exploits is
but to establish a tyranny—*Infelix, quanta dominum virtute parasti!*

[1] Housman punctures this idea, p. 327. For Mars as a malignant planet, see Ptol., *Tetr.* 1. 5.
[2] Cf. Ovid, *Met.* 11. 69: Hor., *Od.* 1. 12. 6: Sen., *Oed.* 434–5.
[3] Yet there is room for poetry—e.g. *Pangaea nivosis cana iugis* (recalling Horace's Soracte).
and *Alpis nubiferae colles atque aeriam Pyrenen.*
[4] Perhaps this vision presents a prospectus of Lucan's completed poem: see Getty's notes
(ed. of book 1), however, for a different interpretation of *nova litora ponti* (693).

The direct inspiration of the matron looks forward to the episode of the Delphic oracle (5. 71–236).

The story of Appius was evidently popular as an *exemplum* for declaimers, and the details in Lucan are in many respects similar to those in Valerius Maximus.[1] This may account for the impression of triteness which the episode cannot disguise; to this reader, at any rate, it carries less conviction than the passages in books 1 and 6, except for the speculative passage at 86–101. Book 5 opens with a meeting of the senators in Pompey's camp and the speech of the consul, Lentulus, proposing that Pompey be given the supreme command. This is followed by the handing out of rewards and recognition to allied princes, including Ptolemy: thus the seeds are sown whose harvest will be the murder of Pompey. With this irony the meeting disperses, and the leaders prepare for war, ignorant of their fate: by contrast, Appius, consul in 54 and now governor of Achaea, determines to find what destiny awaits him. His inquiry, as we find out, only misleads him; but it is sufficient for Lucan as a peg on which to hang his excursus on Delphi and inspired prophecy.

After a brief passage on Delphi and its mythology (71–85) Lucan considers the question of inspiration (86–101). His explanation is the Stoic doctrine: whether Fate is objective and predictable, or whether the divine word by its utterance ordains the future (92–3), the divine element is immanent in the world, its support and motive principle. This element finds egress from the heart of the earth at certain places—such as Delphi; in the same way, it is active within human beings, and in some persons it creates such a spiritual disturbance that it is forced out and finds expression in human words. The disturbance and the violent outburst of the divine inspiration is like a volcanic eruption (93–101). For others, presumably the majority of men, no such disturbance is necessary or likely: for a few, the self-sufficient philosophers, the divine element is so integrated in them that they know the will of God and have no need of prophecies or divination (see Cato's words at 9. 572–6). Moreover, even if the future is foretold, the prophecy cannot alter the destined course of events (see Erictho's words at 6. 611–15).

So much for speculation: the story now continues as Appius compels the *antistes* to open the Delphic shrine, long closed and

[1] Val. Max., 1. 8. 10. It is impossible to determine whether in fact Lucan went to Livy (Valerius' chief source) for his *exempla* or to Valerius' handbook. The latter appears *prima facie* more likely to the present writer. There are similarities with Valerius in Luc. 67–70; 120–7; 116–20; 194–6; 230–6 (where the geographical names seem to be a certain echo).

silent (Lucan supposes that its silence is the result of tyranny, when the tyrant fears an oracle that will run counter to his wishes, 111–14). The Pythia, **here** given the name Phemonoe ('speaker of thoughts'), herself is unwilling to prophesy; at first she refuses to enter the shrine, and then gives a false answer (102–57). At this Appius threatens her (157–61), a feature of the scene that is comparable to the διαβολή in necromancy (6. 730–49): this drives her to the tripod, and the god takes possession of her (161–93). After her frenzy and the agony of seeing the whole destiny of the world revealed (177–82), the prophecy itself comes as an anti-climax (194–6), unless one supposes that Lucan is contrasting the universal horror involved in the destruction of Roman liberty, on the field of Pharsalia, with the insignificance of the fate of one man. This is implied in the next passage: the Pythia stops short (197) and Lucan gives an apostrophe on partial foreknowledge (198–208)—the fall of the Republic and the death of Pompey are too terrible to be uttered, and the murder of the tyrant (Caesar) must be suppressed, for fear that he should avoid it if it were foretold.

All that remains now is to describe the aftermath, the subsidence of the emotional disturbance in the Pythia and her swoon (208–24). As for Appius, much good the prophecy did him, for he could not escape the death he feared, and soon perished, as the god had obscurely foretold, in Euboea (224–36). With his departure from the scene the story reverts to Caesar who, whatever storms he faces, fears no powers above and knows that he is the favourite and the equal of Fortune.

Lucan had, as Bourgéry remarks, 'l'amour du mystère et le goût du surnaturel', and the Erictho episode is treated with a gusto that is quite lacking in the Delphi passage. The episode is Lucan's *Nekuia*, occupying the central portion of his poem, just as Homer's had in *Odyssey* 11 and Virgil's in *Aeneid* 6.[1] It is necessary in the structure of the poem principally as a prelude to the climax at Pharsalia; it is also inevitable as a counterweight to the Delphic episode, setting the occult practice of necromancy against the inspiration of Apollo (cf. 6. 770–3). Wisely Lucan deliberately contrasts his *nekuia* with those of Homer and Virgil: he describes superstition, not religion; his inquirer is not an Odysseus or an Aeneas, but Sextus Pompeius, the unworthy son of a great father (6. 420);[2] the guide and interpreter is

---

[1] *Nekuia* nearly contemporary with Lucan's are at Statius, *Theb.* 4. 406–645: Silius, 13. 381–895.

[2] In fact Sextus was sent to Mitylene with Cornelia (Plut., *Pomp.* 66); see *R.E.* 21, col. 2214–5.

not a Teiresias, a Sibyl or an Anchises, but a witch capable of every
sort of foul crime and unfit to live with other human beings (6.
507–13). No rational account of the Underworld, compatible with
Stoic doctrine is attempted; finally, the utterance of the dead man
(777–820), far from presenting a pageant of Rome's future greatness
(*Aen.* 6. 756–853), brings onto the stage the demagogues who had
destroyed the Roman constitution and foretells the immediate end
of Roman law and liberty.

The episode is very long; it is morbid, sensational, hyperbolical.
It is usually dismissed as mere rhetoric: yet it is still a careful account
of the practice of necromancy, the fullest in Latin literature. It is
therefore worth while digressing in order to survey the various
influences to which Lucan may have been subjected in composing
the episode.

In Greek literature Circe (*Od.* 10. 210 sqq.) and Medea are the
supreme witches. Euripides' *Medea* is more of a psychological study
of Medea's predicament than a description of her magic; Sophocles
evidently was more concerned with the magic in his 'Ριζοτόμοι
(Dindorf fr. 479–81), in which Medea's herbs and magic brew were
described (Macrobius, *Sat.* 5. 19) and the invocation to Hecate was
made. Sophron wrote a mime about sorceresses, and Menander
wrote a *Thessalian Woman* which included the formula for 'drawing
down the moon' (Pliny, *N.H.* 30. 7). Of the Alexandrians, Theo-
critus' second *Idyll* is the supreme example of love-magic; Apollo-
nius, however, does not appear to have taken advantage of the
opportunities afforded him by his subject.[1] Other miscellaneous
Greek magic passages are to be found in Hesiod (invocation to
Hecate, *Theog.* 411 sqq.), the Orphic myths, and the magic papyri.
These last provide confirmation of Lucan's ritual and show that his
episode is not merely literary in its conception.

Much of this finds its way into Roman literature: Ennius adapted
the *Medea* of Euripides, and was followed by Pacuvius and Accius.
Ovid's tragedy on Medea was praised by Quintilian (10. 1. 98) and
Tacitus (*Dial.* 12), while he wrote two other studies of her (*Her.* 12;
Met. 7. 1–403), of which the *Metamorphoses* passage is among the
most important sources for Lucan's magic. Nor will Lucan himself
have failed to be influenced by Seneca's *Medea*; and his own early
interest in the occult is attested by a *Medea* (unfinished, according to
Vacca), a work on Orpheus and a *Catachthonion* (cf. Statius, *Silv.*

---

[1] Passages on magic at 3. 802–9; 843–66; 1029–45; 1201–20; 4. 1661–72.

F

2. 7. 57–9). Too well known to need discussion here are Virgil's eighth *Eclogue*, his African witch (*Aen.* 4. 483–91) and Horace's Canidia (*Epodes* 5 and 17; *Sat.* 1. 8). For the rites of necromancy Seneca's *Oedipus* (530–658) is in some respects close to Lucan: it is one of the few passages where a man is the principal.[1]

As for the declamations, although poisoning is a frequent theme and ghosts have their place, the similarities with Lucan lie more in the manner than the matter. Five of the Senecan declamations deal with poisoning (*Contr.* 3. 7; 6. 4 and 6; 7. 3; 9. 6), and there is little in them that has direct bearing on Lucan: the emphasis is more on the motives of the poisoner (Virgil's *iniusta noverca* in a new guise) than the horror of her arts. However, when Silo declines to outline the typical poisoner for his audience (*Contr.* 9. 6. 14) he implies that such descriptions were habitual. Of the later declamations, six of pseudo-Quintilian and four of Calpurnius deal with poison;[2] there are some quite horrific descriptions of poisoned corpses (e.g. *Decl. Mai.* 15. 4; *Decl. Min.* 354, synopsis). In the *Gladiator* (*Decl. Mai.* 9. 7) the dead man's ghost appears; in the *Sepulcrum incantatum* (*Decl. Mai.* 10) a magician is summoned to lay a ghost by putting spells on a tomb, and here too the ghost appears. The spells are mentioned but not quoted: in the peroration Pluto is addressed, but it is feeble stuff compared with the red meat of Lucan (e.g. 6. 744 sqq.).

Of all these literary influences, it is clear that Ovid and Seneca are the most important for Lucan's magic; Virgil for his conception of the place of the episode in an epic. It will become evident later that Lucan's knowledge of the ritual goes far beyond that of Ovid and that he must either have attended magical seances or have consulted handbooks on the subject, similar to the magic papyri. And what may be summed up as the 'climate of opinion' should not be forgotten—the interest in the occult that was inherent in the superstitious Roman character and the influences (particularly from the East) to which Rome lay open in the first century A.D. There is plenty of evidence for the practice of magic rites at Rome throughout her history,[3] and among the sources of such activities three appear to be particularly important—Etruria, Greece and Egypt. The tomb-paintings at Tarquinii are sufficient evidence of the

---

[1] Cf. Pliny, *N.H.* 25. 10. Other examples of a male principal are Moeris (Virg., *Ecl.* 8. 96), and Petronius, *Sat.* 61–2: in both cases he is a werewolf.

[2] Ps. Quint., *Decl. Mai.* 14, 15, 17; *Decl. Min.* 354, 377, 381: Calp., 12, 13, 35, 40.

[3] E.g. Pliny, *N.H.* 30. 12 (97 B.C.); 28. 2 (the Twelve Tables: cf. Aug., *Civ. Dei* 8. 19): Aug., *Civ. Dei* 7. 35 (quoting Varro on Numa).

development of chthonic superstitions during the time of the late Republic; the monstrous demons, such as Tuculcha in the Tomb of Orcus, are but a short step from Virgil's Tisiphone or Lucan's Erictho. More significant yet was the importance which the Etruscans attached to blood, especially in the ritual fight between human combatants whose blood, drenching the ground, was an offering to the spirit of the dead man whose funeral was being celebrated. Such was the religious origin of the gladiatorial fights; it would not be fanciful to see a connection in Lucan between Scaeva in the earlier part of book 6 (his deeds must have had a close connection with Lucan's own visits to the amphitheatre) and the rites of Erictho which follow soon after.[1]

According to Pliny (N.H. 24. 156) it was the Greek philosophers who introduced the eastern science of herbal magic to the west; in a number of passages (24. 160; 25. 13–14; 30. 9–10) he names Democritus and Pythagoras as particularly involved in this. At this point the revival of Pythagoreanism at Rome by Nigidius Figulus becomes relevant, for it certainly included magic as well as astrology. Cicero charges Vatinius with unspeakable magic rites practised under the cloak of Neophythagoreanism (In Vat. 14); these included summoning of ghosts and sacrifice of children.[2] Varro (quoted by Augustine, Civ. Dei 7. 35) is the authority for Pythagoras himself practising necromancy; evidently Nigidius and his friends did the same, so that he could be dismissed as Pythagoricus et Magus (Jerome) and his school as the sodalicium sacrilegi Nigidiani (ps.-Cic., In Sall. 14). Lucan's interest in Nigidius may have been one of the sources of his necromancy.

As for Egypt, the Alexandrian professor of rhetoric, Apion, had a vogue at Rome in the reign of Tiberius: he talked of evocation of the dead, but Pliny (N.H. 30. 18) thought him an impostor. Others may have been more impressed: certainly Egypt, home of the magical papyri, was a source of the foreign superstitions which Tacitus refers to (Ann. 11. 15) as growing at Rome in the reign of Claudius; necromancy will have been among these.

Tacitus, indeed, provides more concrete evidence for the occult under the Julio-Claudians. When Germanicus lay dying in A.D. 19, it was said that he had been poisoned by Piso and traces of exhumed

---

[1] Perhaps Octavian's slaughter of 300 captured soldiers at the Etruscan city of Perusia in 40 B.C. was a ritual offering. Suetonius, Aug. 15, throws doubt on the whole story with his scribunt quidam.

[2] Cf. C.I.L. vi. 19747 for the epitaph of an infant killed by a witch (time of Tiberius): the straw changeling in Petr., Sat. 63: Juv., Sat. 6. 550–2: Luc., 6. 710.

corpses were found, together with spells and curses and 'other things
which are believed to be used in devoting souls to the powers of the
underworld' (*Ann.* 2. 69. 5). When Libo Drusus was tried for sedi-
tion, the trial only came on when a certain Junius gave information
that he had been approached to help in raising some ghosts: at the
trial, the evidence consisted solely of *libelli vaecordes* saying that Libo
had consulted people about his future wealth, and of a paper in his
own hand listing the names of Caesars and senators with secret signs
marked against them (*Ann.* 2. 28 and 30). In the year of the Pisonian
conspiracy Lepida was accused (among other things) of practising
sinister rites (*Ann.* 16. 8): a few lines later Tacitus describes the
horrors which afflicted Italy that year, especially a plague which
filled 'the houses with corpses and the streets with funerals'. The
times were perfect for necromancers. As for Nero himself, he
attempted necromancy (Pliny, *N.H.* 30. 14–15), but found that it
told him nothing; his indulgence in the occult, unsuccessful as it
was, would inevitably have had its influence. Indeed, there are so
many similarities between Suetonius on Nero's superstitions (*Nero*
56) and Lucan on Sextus (6. 419–34), that it may be wondered if
Nero was not the real subject of Lucan's portrait.

Such is the background to the Erictho episode. By line 332 of
book 6 the rival armies are making for Thessaly, about to pitch
camp for the great encounter. A description of the land is called
for (333–412), which Ovid in his Medea story had introduced in the
guise of a nine-day tour by Medea in search of herbs (*Met.* 7. 192–
237. At 413 the interest turns for a few lines to the combatants,
among whom is Sextus: his fears and his predilection for black magic
lead on to another excursus, this time upon Thessalian magic (434–
91), followed by a speculative passage (492–9) on the relationship
between the gods and witchcraft (in this case Lucan is less conclusive
than in the similar passage in the Delphi episode, 5. 86–101): in
conclusion Lucan adds a few lines (499–506) on the spectacular
Thessalian magic of drawing down the moon.

Thus by the time Erictho is introduced (507–68) the reader is
thoroughly acquainted with Thessaly and its witches, and Lucan is
able to make his sustained hyperbole (of Erictho as beginning where
the other witches leave off) more persuasive: the keynote of the
description of her magic is the epigram at 560, *hominum mors omnis
in usu est*—suitably portentous for the eve of Pharsalia, and that this
link with the main story is in Lucan's mind is shown by the follow-
ing paragraph (569–87), where Erictho is anticipating the carnage of

Pharsalia. At last (588–623) Sextus interviews her and makes his request, which is to know who is fated to die in the coming campaign: her reply asserts that even she is lesser than Fate (here is the note of certainty missing from the speculative passage at 492–9) but that she can obtain knowledge of the future, unalterable as it will be.

Thus the magic begins, and it must be admitted that the length of Lucan's preparation (nearly 200 lines) in some measure defeats its own ends, for the *tour de force* of the ritual itself inevitably loses some of its impact when it is so long delayed. At any rate, Erictho first chooses her corpse to bring back to life (624–41): it must be one of a φθίμενος ἄωρος, for these, having died before their allotted span of life is fulfilled, have not yet been allowed to enter the underworld (cf. 712–15; 777–9); caught, as it were, between the two worlds, they are in the best position to have knowledge of affairs in both.[1] The setting is suitable: the black Thessalian night is made doubly dark by the witch (624) and even the birds and beasts of prey cannot bear her presence. The landscape for the ritual itself would satisfy the most morbid romantic—cliffs, yew-trees, cavernous and dank darkness (642–51). Dressed in her witch's garb Erictho, with a few defiant words, is ready to begin her *cuisine magique* (642–66): the corpse is prepared and the ingredients of her brew (which make *Macbeth* pale in comparison) prepared (667–84). So far Lucan has followed Ovid and in places (e.g. Luc. 679 from Ovid, *Met.* 7. 272) borrowed from him: but Ovid lost interest once the preparations were finished. For him, Medea's incantation is a *murmur longum* (251), and with a few perfunctory lines (285–93) he rejuvenates Aeson and brings the séance to its end.[2]

Not so Lucan. The brew is but part of the spell; it is ineffective without the incantation. Erictho's voice contains the sound of every beast of ill-omen, all the threatening sounds that nature knows (685–94), as the powers of Hell are invoked to bring back to life the dead man (695–718). Despite the repetition of gruesome details, the passage has considerable power: Lucan combines a detailed knowledge of the magic ἀγωγὴ ἐπὶ βιαίων with enthusiasm for his subject, and the effect is far removed from the literary fancies of Ovid or Seneca.

Yet Erictho's spells are not enough to bend the powers of the Underworld to her will, and the ghost is reluctant to enter its body a second time (719–24): the magician's most mighty weapon must

[1] See Cumont, *After-Life* (59 , note 1), 133–4 cf. Virg., *Aen.* 3. 379–80.
[2] See Fahz (*op. cit.*, 59 , note 1), 55–60, for details of similarities between Lucan and Ovid.

be employed, the threat that will compel compliance (725–49); its
climax is the appeal to the great nameless deity. At this the corpse
comes to life (750–62) and Erictho commands it to speak, binding it
to answer her requests with a further spell (762–76).

The ritual is over and what is virtually a new scene begins; for
the prophecy, to which the ritual has been leading, brings the
reader back to the theme of the epic: it is the immediate prelude to
the catastrophe of the next book (776–820). The dead man weeps,
and his message is more a lament for Rome than a prophecy ad-
dressed to the individual, Sextus. He reports what he has seen and
heard at the entrance to the underworld: there too civil war has
divided the Roman shades. Before him passed two groups; the
blessed were sad, but the criminals and those who had attacked their
country were rejoicing. Pluto himself is preparing to receive the
victor in the war into everlasting punishment, while Pompey and
his sons will join the blessed dead; however humiliated they will
have been on earth, they will then be able to trample on the *Roma-
norum manes deorum*, the shades of the deified Caesars. As for the
protagonists, both will die, the one in Egypt, the other in Rome;
Sextus himself will learn his fate later from his father's ghost (evi-
dently Pompey's ghost would have appeared in the later part of the
poem, which Lucan did not live to complete). The prophecy ends
on an ironic note—Pompey and his sons will die in the three lands
(Africa, Spain, Asia) over which he had triumphed.

The prophecy is 'Roman' and patriotic; it owes much to Virgil
and at the same time is the antithesis of his theme. The dead man
claims only partial knowledge (777) and leaves surer knowledge of
the future to a better-informed prophet. So Helenus claimed only
partial foreknowledge (*Aen.* 3. 456–60) and refers Aeneas to the
Sibyl. In Lucan, Pompey's ghost would have surveyed the loss of
Rome's liberty and the fall of the Republic: his theme, the rise of
tyranny, would have been in contrast to the prophecy of Anchises
in the *Aeneid*. Even in the present passage, however, the contrast
with Anchises is clear enough: in the *Aeneid* (6. 824–35) a cavalcade
of Roman heroes passed by, followed by Caesar and Pompey—the
climax of the passage being the *Aeneid's* only reference to the Civil
War:

> ne pueri, ne tanta animis adsuescite bella
> neu patriae validas in viscera vertite viris;
> tuque prior, tu parce, genus qui ducis Olympo,
> proice tela manu, sanguis meus!

This is Lucan's model and his context: Rome's greatness is to pass away, and the heroes of the Republic—the Decii, Camillus, Curius, Scipio and Cato—lament. Even Sulla (elsewhere in Lucan a bloodthirsty tyrant) is included: at least his cognomen, *Felix*, denoted Rome's good fortune, and that now must change. Only Brutus rejoices—and here is a glimpse of the murder of Caesar.[1] Conversely the bad citizens rejoice, and their names go backward in time: from Catiline and Marius the survey passes to the source of the trouble, the demagogues like Drusus and the Gracchi whose ambition first undermined the authority of the Senate and weakened the constitution of the Republic.[2]

The climax has been reached: the Republic must fall and Pompey be killed. All that remains is to restore the corpse to death a second time and escort Sextus back to the Pompeian camp (820-30). The times indeed are out of joint; fittingly the book closes with unnatural night and the seventh opens with a late and sorrowful dawn. The destiny of Rome approaches its catastrophe.

In conclusion, we may find Lucan's mature views on divination in book 9. Cato's march takes him to the oracle of Ammon; here Labienus, an unstable man (for he had deserted Caesar), encourages Cato to consult the god. His speech, virtually a *suasoria* (9. 550-63), argues that here is an unrivalled opportunity to know the future; Cato, pure and holy and closest to God in his life, is particularly suited to talk with Jupiter. Cato, whose reply is itself oracular (564-5), refuses. He dismisses the various questions he could ask the oracle; in each case the answer is obvious to the Stoic. Should he live or die under a tyranny? Should he worry at the prospect of an early death? Should he, conscious of his virtue, be afraid of Fortune's slings and arrows? He needs no external encouragement, for the virtuous man knows the truth; unshaken he can face all that may happen, able in the end to face Death, the one certainty in life (566-84).

Here is the Stoic belief, Lucan's ideal view. But for Lucan the fascination of the occult was strong, and the dramatic possibilities were too inviting. Not all men are as Cato and lesser mortals are fearful and need encouragement for the future. The inquirers in his

---

[1] For *exempla* of Roman patriots cf. Luc., 7. 358-60. Virgil's lists are at *Georg.* 2. 169-70, *Aen.* 6. 824-6.

[2] Cf. Pompey's speech at Luc., 2. 541-6: in Virgil, *Aen.* 6. 824, 842, the names of Drusus and Gracchus were honourable.

divination episodes are quite un-Stoic: the fearful people of Rome (1. 673), the coward, Appius (5. 67–8), Sextus, unworthy son of his father, driven by fear to know the future (6. 423). Here was Lucan's opportunity—and who was he to refuse the chance thus presented, so rich in dramatic and rhetorical potentiality?

CHAPTER VI

LUCAN'S DREAMS

THE Erictho episode and the sixth book had ended in unnatural darkness. Book 7 opens with an equally unnatural dawn, but quickly (lines 7 sqq.) returns to the events of the night, in particular Pompey's dream. We now turn to examine Lucan's use of dreams, the last of our rhetorical-poetical themes. We have already seen that Lucan's enthusiasm for the occult led him to compromise in composing his historical epic so as to include long sections on supernatural affairs. Lucan goes yet further in refusing to discard the standard epic device of dreams, the means by which gods often communicated with men: there are three dreams in the poem, as well as a waking vision which fulfils the function of an epic dream.[1] Yet he is not thereby introducing the *deorum ministeria*: there is no vision of a god, such as Aeneas' of Mercury (*Aen.* 4. 554 sqq.). Roma, in Caesar's vision, is no more than a personification of an abstract idea: in the other visions it is the dead who appear twice, and in the third the sleeper sees his own past. The visions serve a different purpose from the traditional epic one: they are necessary to the structure of the poem, and they are essential to its rhetoric in being *par excellence* devices for the manipulation of *color*.[2]

Whether Lucan's work is considered from the poetic, historical, philosophical or rhetorical standpoint, there was plenty of precedent to make it clear that it would have been bold indeed to abandon so well-established a feature. It is sufficient merely to mention here the long tradition, from Homer onwards, of dreams in epic writing (for others have dealt with this aspect of the subject). For historians, dreams were almost as necessary: Livy certainly had a predilection for them, and one at least of Lucan's dreams was originally related

---

[1] 1. 185 (Caesar's vision of Roma); 3. 8 (Pompey's vision of Julia); 7. 7 (Pompey's dream of his theatre); 7. 760 (visions of Caesar's army after Pharsalia).

[2] The following books and articles are useful: F. Fürbringer, *De somniis in Romanorum poetarum carminibus narratis* (Jena, 1912)—very little discussion: J. G. Wetzel, *Quomodo poetae epici et Graeci et Romani somnia descripserint* (Berlin, 1931): H. Steiner, *Der Traum in der Aeneis* (Berne, *Noctes Romanae* 5, 1952): H. J. Rose, 'The Dream of Pompey', *Acta Classica* 1 (1958), 80 sqq.: W. Rutz, 'Die Träume des Pompeius in Lucans *Pharsalia*', *Hermes* 91 (1963), 334–45. I have not been able to obtain J. B. Stearns, *Studies of the Dream as a Technical Device in Latin Epic and Drama* (Lancaster, Pa., 1927). For general information; T. Hopfner, art. 'Traumdeutung', *R-E.* ser. 2, vol. 6, col. 2233: A. S. Pease, ed. of Cicero, *De Divinatione* (Urbana, Illinois, 1920–3).

by him.[1] Historical dreams were firmly rooted in the tradition; the Hellenistic writers set the fashion, and enthusiastic purveyors of dreams such as Coelius (one of Livy's sources) were happy to ignore the criticisms of more sober historians such as Polybius (see Pol., 12. 24. 5).[2] Dreams, then, would not be out of place in historical epic.

There is little speculation about the explanation of dreams in Lucan's dream-writing: even the passage at 7. 19–24 has pathos as its primary aim. It is clear that Lucan was himself sceptical about dreams as a method of divination, and would have had serious reservations in accepting the Stoic doctrine on dreams.[3] According to this, the mind was freed by sleep from the limitations of the body, and in this state was able to remember the past, observe the present and foresee the future (Cic., De Div. 1. 63)—those who are close to death having the greater power of foresight. So far this would have been acceptable: but Posidonius (ibid. 64) went further—it was the influence of the gods that made men dream, and this in three ways. Either the mind had its own powers of foresight; or it had visions of immortal souls (of which there are very many in the upper air) who have in them 'the marks of truth'; or it was directly addressed by the gods. Such divine apparatus certainly had no place in Lucan's poem, and probably none in his own beliefs either: better, then, to use dreams entirely as a dramatic device.

In this he was supported by his training. There had been handbooks of dreams (as, for example, that of Chrysippus—Cic., De Div. 2. 134) among the Greeks and the fashion was followed by the Romans—for example, the list of dreams in Valerius Maximus (1. 7): the declaimer Junius Otho published four books of colores which were so full of dreams that Gallio called them 'Antiphon-books'.[4] It was as a device for the use of color that the dream was an important weapon in the orator's armoury: while the dream makes the hearer more aware of the significance of the ensuing action, it can excite sympathy for or hostility towards the dreamer. This evidently was

---

[1] See P. G. Walsh, Livy (Cambridge, 1961), 131. Cf. Herodotus' belief in dreams (e.g. 5. 55).

[2] Dreams from Coelius are quoted by Cicero, De Div. 1. 39, 48, 49, 55, 56. See Cic., De Div. 1. 55 for dreams and the annalists: ibid. 51 for dreams and the official records.

[3] Expounded in Cic., De Div. 1. 39–65 criticized, ibid. 2. 119–50.

[4] Sen., Contr. 2. 1. 33. For Antiphon (an interpreter of dreams, fl. c. 400 B.C.) cf. Cic., De Div. 1. 39 and 116; 2. 144. He should probably be distinguished from Antiphon the orator (see Wellmann, R-E., 1.2. col. 2529, s.v. 'Antiphon', no. 15).

overdone by many declaimers: Seneca Rhetor implies that excessive use of dreams was an instance of the degeneracy of rhetoric (*Contr.* 2. 1. 33), and more than a generation later Quintilian dismisses *somniorum colores* as worthless, so easy were they to introduce.[1]

All the same, it is for their use of *color* that Lucan's four visions are most significant. They are arranged in pairs, and concern only Pompey and Caesar. Caesar's vision of Roma is balanced by Pompey's of Julia: the one prepares for Caesar's hostile entry into the fatherland, the other accompanies Pompey's final departure from Italy. In Book 7 the two visions contrast the two leaders and their relationship with the Roman people: the one precedes the action of the crisis, the other is associated with the closing of the scene. Again, the visions are significant in the development of the protagonists' characters: the theme of Caesar's visions is *furor* (7. 776–80), and they mark the progress of his corruption, first as he kindles the flame of war (1. 204 and 225), later as his madness reaches its climax on the field of Pharsalia.[2] Pompey's dreams are less dynamic, looking to the past rather than to the present or future: while they are important for the delineation of Pompey's character, they do not mark stages in its development, still less in Pompey's progress towards Stoic perfection.[3] They do, however, underline the pathos inherent in the two crises in the development of Pompey's tragedy —his departure from Italy and the disaster at Pharsalia.

At 1. 185–203 Caesar, on reaching the banks of the Rubicon, sees a vision of Rome herself. The famous episode of the crossing of the Rubicon was variously described: Caesar himself (*B.C.* 1. 8. 1) merely says *Ariminum proficiscitur*, but Plutarch, Appian and Suetonius, whose original source was Asinius (who was present at the crossing, Plut., *Caes.* 32. 5), say more. Caesar hesitated, considering the consequences of his action, and finally crossed with the words ἀνερρίφθω κύβος (Plut., *Caes.* 32; *Pomp.* 60; App., *B.C.* 2. 35). Plutarch adds that Caesar dreamed that he had incestuous intercourse with his mother (possibly here symbolic of Rome or Roman Italy), a dream which Suetonius (*D.J.* 7) had reported as taking place during Caesar's quaestorship of Spain, in 67 B.C. Appian adds a list

---

[1] Quint., 4. 2. 94: cf. Petr., *Sat.* 10. For *loci contra somnia* see Sen., *Suas.* 4. 4.

[2] 7. 786–96. A dream could have been expected at the next stage, Caesar's visit to Egypt: instead, Pompey's ghost is introduced (10. 6–7), which provides the element of the supernatural, while the Alexander-diatribe (10. 20–52) provides the *color*.

[3] This is the view of B. M. Marti, 'The Meaning of the *Pharsalia*', *A.J.P.* 66 (1945) 352 sqq. (esp. 367–73). W. Rutz finds Pompey's dreams 'entirely stationary'.

of portents: but only Suetonius, besides Lucan, has the vision of a supernatural being (*D.J.* 32). In Suetonius the apparition (which may indeed have been real, a piece of stage-management by Caesar) sounds a trumpet and crosses the river, giving Caesar his cue to urge his men to do likewise and follow the *deorum ostenta.* Lucan's vision is based on the same story as that of Suetonius: but he needs a personage that will hold Caesar back, not the inflammatory apparition of Suetonius. And so Rome herself appears, recalling the famous personification in Cicero's first Catilinarian speech:[1] turreted, as in Virgil,[2] she appears, not in majesty, but in deep mourning— *maestissima, effundens crines, caesarie lacera, nudis lacertis.*[3] Her request is simple (190–2): no Roman army should march on Rome—'si iure venitis, si cives, huc usque licet.' For a moment Caesar pauses, irresolute:[4] then his country's prayer is brushed aside and he appeals to the gods of Rome and to Roma herself in self-justification (195– 203). In other words, he has put his own *dignitas* before his country's good—*ille erit, ille nocens, qui me tibi fecerit hostem* (cf. Caesar himself, at *B.C.* 1. 7–9). The speech is rich in irony: Caesar includes in his prayer the gods of Rome from the earliest days (Juppiter Latiaris, worshipped at Alba Longa) down to Roma, the symbol of Augustus' revitalized national religion (Lucan may be forgiven the anachronism), and he puts himself above them all. The words *fave coeptis* belong rightly in a prayer at the founding of a city, not at its destruction: they are used by Pompey (8. 322) as he proposes to use the Parthians as allies against Caesar. The implication there is that whichever side wins, one or other of the two great disasters which destroyed the Republic (Carrhae and Pharsalia) will be avenged:[5] either way it will be a renewal of hope, even a refounding, for the Roman Republic. Equally ironically (to return to 1. 200) Caesar denies that he comes *furialibus armis*: yet he is about to unleash civil war, supreme *furor* in a citizen.

[1] Cic., *In Cat.* 1. 18 and 27: quoted by Quint., 9. 2. 32, as an example of prosopopoeia.

[2] *Aen.* 6. 781–7: cf. Lucr., 2. 606–7. Similar descriptions in Varro (*ap.* Aug., *Civ. Dei,* 7. 24): Ovid, *Fast.* 4. 219–20 6. 321: Prop., 3. 17. 35.

[3] The effect is increased by the accumulation of epithets between *visa* (186) and its dependent *adstare* (188) cf. 1. 9–12. The Schol. Bern. on 1. 189 comments: 'erubesce Caesar. viso te Roma non loqui sed flere conpellitur.'

[4] 192–4. *Horror,* etc., is the regular consequence of a literary vision: cf. Virg., *Aen.* 2. 774. Sen., *Tro.* 457: *Octavia,* 123, 735–6.

[5] 8. 325–7: 'cum Caesaris arma / concurrent Medis, aut me fortuna necesse est / vindicet aut Crassos.' In 1. 8–12, however, Lucan suggests that the Romans should have united against the Parthians and this, rather than the views attributed to Pompey, may be taken as more representative of Republican sentiment.

The scene is completed by the majestic simile of the lion (205-12), emphasizing Caesar's *ira*;[1] and by the description of the crossing itself (213-26). As Caesar sets foot on the Italian bank he cries:

'hic', ait, 'hic pacem temerataque iura relinquo;
te, Fortuna, sequor; procul hinc iam foedera sunto;
credidimus fatis, utendum est iudice bello.'[2]

No longer will the ways of peace be his means to justice, but war; no longer will the moral law be his guide, but Fortune.

With this, the first mention of Caesar's Fortune in the poem, the meaning of the vision is made clear. By it Lucan is, firstly, signifying the solemnity of the moment and the importance of Caesar's decision; secondly, Caesar and his country are brought face to face. Finally, this confrontation gives the *color* for the presentation of a general who leads his army not for his country but for himself; whose guiding light is to be Fortune. And what does this 'Fortune' mean? Lucan provides the answer (7. 796): *Fortunam superosque suos in sanguine cernit.*

The vision that accompanies Caesar's entry into Italy is balanced by the dream with which Pompey leaves the country for ever (3. 8-35).[3] Its *color* is twofold: the civil war has begun, and therefore Julia has joined the number of the guilty shades, expelled now from the Elysian Fields; in this guilt Pompey must share, for he sealed the fate of the triumvirate by contracting an alliance with the optimate Cornelia, after the deaths of Julia herself and Crassus. Secondly, the contrast is drawn between Pompey's former success and his present decline; the marriage with Cornelia is symbolic of this, for Cornelia had been married to P. Crassus, who fell at Carrhae, the other disaster (besides the death of Julia) that shattered the triumvirate. It is this part of the *color* that is particularly important in the portrait of Pompey; throughout the poem *stat magni nominis umbra* (1. 135) is the key to the portrait, and the desertion by Fortune of her favourite is a leading motif. The dream marks a decisive stage in this process, as can clearly be seen from its context.

Towards the end of book 2 Pompey is shown giving orders to his son, Gnaeus, and to the consuls to sail off and mobilize the support of his allies. The speech to Gnaeus is in essence a survey of

---

[1] Cf. Hom., *Il.* 20. 164-74: Virg., *Aen.* 12. 4-8: Sen., *Oed.* 919-20.
[2] Housman's over-ingenious *satis his* is rejected (for *fatis*). The Schol. Bern. says *iura* refers to the triumvirate, and explains *foedera* as 'aut propinquitatis aut imperii aut legum aut iuris.'
[3] See Rutz *art. cit.* 340-4, who considers the vision to be Lucan's reply to Dido's curse in *Aen.* 4. 615 sqq.

Pompey's eastern conquests (2. 632–44), ending with the *sententia* 'omnes redeant in castra triumphi'. Thus his former glory is brought before the reader: yet vestiges of this greatness remain—Pompey can still give orders to the consuls (2. 645–9); he only has to speak and the highest dignitaries of state obey. But the truth is that Fortune has left him: he prays unsuccessfully to her (2. 699–701) and the book closes, as evening draws on, with Pompey setting sail, still with the trappings of greatness (730), but doomed (725–8). In the final lines (731–6) the poet looks forward to his death: death is never to be far from Lucan's Pompey henceforward, and the vision of Julia introduces the new theme. Indeed, Pompey's immediate reaction to the vision is to renounce his fear of death (3. 38–40).

The scene as the ships set sail for Greece is symbolically drawn: all Pompey's men look ahead to Greece (3. 3), while he himself alone looks back to Italy (3. 4). Cornelia accompanies him in his voyage (2. 728); now he finds that Julia too is with him. As he sinks down to sleep she appears to him, in the guise of a Fury; the Fury's duty was to avenge *impietas*, and it is suitable that his former wife, Caesar's daughter, should remind Pompey of his share in the guilt of bringing about (by his new marriage) the supreme *impietas* of the Civil War.[1] Her message (its opening line, 12, heavy with the long *e* and *o* sounds and the alliteration of *p*) is one of doom. She too must share in the guilt of civil war, a war that will bring death to thousands and punishment to those who have guiltily taken up arms (12–19). As for Pompey, his marriage to Cornelia symbolizes his changed fortune (20–3): even so, he cannot shake his former wife off; he is still hers (note the hyperbole at 28—not even the waters of Lethe can make her forget him) and she will see that he can never forget his relationship to Caesar (24–32). His efforts to erase this relationship by force of arms are futile: the only result will be Pompey's death and his final reunion with Julia (33–4). And with these ominous words, the vision fades, just as Virgil's Creusa, after a very different sort of prophecy, had eluded the grasp of her husband (*Aen.* 2. 790–4).

Thus the knell is tolled for Pompey: the doom that awaits him over the sea from Italy is dramatically indicated, and the future disaster and the past successes are linked. Historically Lucan's use of Julia, as a device to connect past, present and future in Pompey's tragedy, is correct. Though he is always more sympathetic to

---

[1] For Furies in dreams cf. Virg., *Aen.* 5. 636–7 also 4. 469 (simile): *Octavia* 721–3: Luc. 7. 783.

Cornelia (cf. 8. 104), he rightly appreciates the disastrous significance of her death. From Valerius Maximus, 4. 6. 4, we know that it was a rhetorical *exemplum* and one of which Lucan takes full advantage at 1. 111–20. She is the reminder of the tragic consequences of her death: dramatically she is a foil to Cornelia, brought in by Lucan with telling symbolism in the present passage and at 8. 102–5—two crises where Pompey and Cornelia sail across the sea in flight, the first from Italy to Greece and Pharsalia, the second from Lesbos to Egypt and death.

The second pair of visions mark the prelude and the aftermath of the battle of Pharsalia. Book 7 opens with a reluctant sunrise, appropriate to a day of tragedy and disaster. Then follows Pompey's dream (7–44), in which the theme of contrast between his former and his present condition reaches its most intense treatment.[1] A delusive vision (8), it is free from *horror*, looking back to the real triumphs of the past. So in book 1, Pompey had been portrayed as resting on his laurels, enjoying the applause in his theatre and living, so to speak, on the capital of his earlier good fortune (1. 129–35). The dream recalls those lines, while it marks the end of Pompey's life in this world of self-delusion. After it he goes to his downfall sadly but calmly, aware that Fortune has left him (e.g. 7. 85–6; 647–8) and in full knowledge of the realities of his predicament. It both symbolizes and terminates the passive years in which Pompey, relying on his past successes, let slip the opportunity to lead the Republic to a better destiny. Hence the ensuing scene (45–85), in which the republican leaders assail Pompey's deliberate strategy: his only reply can be to lay down the burden of Rome's destiny (110–11) and release the forces that will destroy her (85–90).

In the dream Pompey sees himself in his theatre, received with the acclamation of the whole Roman people, applause such as he had received at the time of his Spanish triumph (9–19). Lucan then discusses the meaning of the dream (19–24), each explanation being full of pathos: the third, that the dream showed that he would never again see Rome (23–4), is most relevant to Lucan's purpose. It leads naturally to a few lines contrasting the happy vision of Pompey's sleep with the cruel realities of the day of battle and the horror

---

[1] See Rutz *art. cit.* 334–40: also Rose *art. cit.*: A. Guillemin, 'L'Inspiration Virgilienne dans la *Pharsale*', R.E.L. 29 (1951), 214 sqq. The dream is reported by Plutarch, *Pomp.* 68. 2: Florus, 2. 13. 45: Jul. Obs., 65a (the tradition stems from Livy). From Asinius comes another dream, that Pompey dedicated a temple to Venus Victrix (Plut., *ibid.* App., *B.C.* 2. 68).

of its ensuing night (24–8); this is the context for a sustained pane-
gyric (29–44) on Rome's love for Pompey. The reader inevitably
recalls Caesar's confrontation with Roma: his answer to the tears
of the goddess had been a speech of arrogant self-justification. Here
Pompey and Rome are presented in a romantic light: their relation-
ship can only be described by the vocabulary of love (e.g. 32). Pathos
is achieved especially by the use of antithesis—the contrast between
past and present, Rome's expectation and disappointment, Pompey's
triumphs and Caesar's,[1] the applause of the theatre and grief of the
mourners.[2] This is the republican poet's real leave-taking of Pompey,
who (for him) embodied Rome's last hopes of liberty, and it is the
more effective for being placed here, before the catastrophe has
occurred. Whatever the historical truth may be, the passage is
among the finest in the poem for its intensity and pathos: rhetoric
and tragedy are eloquently united.[3]

   The sublimity of Pompey's dream is countered by the hyperboli-
cal virulence of the visions which assail Caesar and his army after
the battle (7. 760–86). According to Caesar, his men went on, after
the capture of the Pompeian camp, the same day to cut off the
Pompeians in the hills and to force them to surrender that evening
and the next morning (Caes., B.C. 3. 96–8).[4] He implies that he
urged them to concentrate on the main task, that of mopping up
the enemy, although they wished to stay and plunder the camp
(ibid. 97), incensed as they were by the luxurious fittings and the
quantities of silver which they found there (the latter, according to
the Pompeians and Lucan, 7. 753, collected to pay for the war).
In Lucan Caesar urges his men to plunder the camp (7. 731–60);
they sleep there in the nobles' quarters and are tormented by visions
of those whom they have killed; next day Caesar feasts in full view

---

[1] In fact Caesar did not celebrate a triumph for Pharsalia.

[2] In 44 planxere is used παρὰ προσδοκίαν for plausere (cf. 7. 12). Note the alliteration of p:
examples of this in S. F. Bonner, Roman Declamation (Liverpool, 1949), 66, the extreme being
at Sen., Contr. 2. 1. 37. In Lucan it seems to be used largely for pathos, e.g. 7. 555 cf. 7. 57,
467–9, 708. For another view of popular applause see Lucan at 9. 215–17. In 43, dolores
(nom.) for dolorem must be read (see A. Hudson-Williams in C.Q. (N.S.) 4. (48), 1954, 187–8):
'whose grief swallowed down their groans'. Thus the silent grief is contrasted with loud
applause. The Loeb translation (gemitus as subject) is meaningless.

[3] For quite a different technique see Cato's speech on Pompey, 9. 190–214 (discussed above,
pp. 5–7). The rhetorical polish of the present passage is indicated by the large number of
figures and tropes used—examples are alliteration and assonance at 27, 41, 43, 44: anaphora,
27, 40–1, 42: antithesis, 26, 33–4, 41–2: isocolon, 37–9 there are many more. Note too the
symmetry of 26 (adj., adj., noun, copula, noun, adj., adj.): cf. 3. 552 for similar technique.

[4] Cf. Plut., Caes. 46 Pomp. 72. 4: App., B.C. 2. 81 and 88. 1. For perversion and suppression
of the truth by Lucan and Caesar see the provocative article by M. Rambaud, 'L'Apologie de
Pompée par Lucain au Livre vii de la Pharsale', R.E.L. 33 (1955), 258.

of the dead, over whom he gloats; he denies them burial (7. 786–824).

Neither account is wholly true: it is the victor's privilege to write the history of the war (or, as Lucan put it into Caesar's mouth, *haec acies victum factura nocentem est*) while Lucan's version makes no effort whatever to disguise his bias. Yet many of the facts were not disputed;[1] therefore the *color* of Lucan's account is of the greatest importance. He is concerned to show that Caesar is guilty of breaking every human and divine law, driven on by madness to commit his crimes. Guilt is the theme that runs through the book, and it is especially the key to the nocturnal visions which are an essential part of the *color*.[2] All Caesar's men are guilty; but while the soldiers suffer for the crimes each individually has committed, Caesar bears the total guilt of his army; his, above all, is the *mens conscia* (784).

All this is foreshadowed: Caesar's speech before the battle (7. 250–329) harps on the theme of guilt (e.g. 260–3); even the clemency of *civis, qui fugerit, esto* (319) is a sham, for Caesar goes on to urge his men, so long as the enemy face them, to trample on the laws of *pietas* (319–25).[3] Later, as the battle was about to begin, the opposing lines stood still, the men recognizing their relatives in the hostile ranks (460–75): it was a Caesarian who broke the moment of conscience and hurled the javelin which launched the slaughter. In the battle it is the Caesarians who strike the blows—the Pompeians are the innocent sufferers (501–3). Caesar himself is depicted as a Fury or as Bellona herself, whipping his troops on to commit more crimes (557–81): where he is, there is a *nox ingens scelerum*.

It is clear that the night after the battle will bring its retribution; the camp, in which Caesar had promised his men they would sleep after the battle (327–8), will be the scene of the punishment of the guilty minds. The Furies are invoked, whose duty it is especially to punish those who have sinned against the laws of *pietas*; the whole apparatus of the Underworld assails Caesar.[4] Thus the scene is

---

[1] Common to all authorities are the capture of the camp and its luxurious appointments: the fact that no mercy was shown to the provincials in Pompey's army, but that no Romans were killed except those carrying arms (Cic., *Pro Lig.* 19, as against Cass. Dio, 41. 62). Suet., *D.J.* 30. 4 and Plut., *Caes.* 46. 1, imply that the Pompeian dead were not buried.

[2] See, for example, 751, 760, 763, 766, 768.

[3] Lucan is perverting the two sayings attributed to Caesar at the battle (Florus, 2. 13. 50): *miles, faciem feri* and *parce civibus*. For the *impietas* cf. 7. 550–1: 'ille locus fratres habuit, locus ille parentes. / Hic furor, hic rabies, hic sunt tua crimina, Caesar.'

[4] 785: *ingestaque Tartara somnis*: perhaps Lucan was thinking of Sen., *H.F.* 89–98. Seneca had a penchant for Furies: see *Ag.* 759 sqq. *Thy.* 40, 78, 250 *Med.* 13–15 *H.F.* 86–8. Cf. also Cic., *Rosc. Am.* 24. 67.

G

unfolded: the troops, guilty and plebeian, sleep in the quarters of the innocent nobles (760–3).[1] They see visions of the relatives whom they have killed (764–76): the horrors are described first in general terms, while Nature herself is in sympathy with the men's *vaesana quies*; then each man is visited by the *Manes* of his victims, in the guise of Furies. The climax is the torment of Caesar himself (776–86): only a double simile from mythology (cf. *Aen.* 4. 469–73) can do justice to it—Orestes had been guilty of impiety towards his parent, Pentheus and Agave of impiety towards the gods: added point is given by the paradoxical antithesis of *fureret* and *desisset*: the one saw the Furies at the height of his madness, the other only when she had returned to her senses. And so Caesar's *horror* will continue into the future: the poet glimpses his assassination and, in the final hyperbole, the murder of Pompey.

Even now Lucan cannot release his readers: in something of an anticlimax Caesar's reaction is given, typically impious and in this recalling his defiance of the superhuman powers in the great storm. Far from feeling remorse, he revels in his crime (786–99), feasting his eyes next day upon the sight of the dead. Once again his *furor* is given full rein: we may well wonder how Lucan would have dealt with the final retribution on the Ides of March.[2]

---

[1] 760–1 are based on Cic., *Phil.* 2. 27 (quoted by Quint., 8. 4. 25, as an example of *amplificatio*): Cicero's pathos is the more effective.

[2] Of the minor characters in the poem, Cornelia dreams at 5. 808–10 and 8. 43–5 (cf., for these, Ovid, *Met.* 11. 471–?, 674–5; Virg., *Aen.* 6. 520). See R. T. Bruère, 'Lucan's Cornelia', *C.P.* 46 (1951), esp. 225–6 with note 62.

Chapter VII

CONCLUSION: LUCAN AND RHETORICAL EPIC

WE may now reconsider Quintilian's estimate with which these studies began: in it Quintilian recommends Lucan as a model for orators rather than poets. Is Quintilian's criticism justified in the light of our studies? Or would it be truer to say that when one has considered Lucan's rhetoric, there is still something left which may justify Lucan's claim to be included among the poets?

Of Lucan's rhetorical mastery there can be no doubt; we have seen in the opening chapter how familiar is his use of the tools of the orator—the divisions of a speech, the figures and tropes, the *color* and *sententiae*—and the skill with which these are handled is apparent in the rhetorical themes which we have examined. Macaulay commented on the extraordinary achievement of so young a man who had 'a complete mastery of political and philosophical rhetoric'. Quintilian, more accurately, found this mastery in Lucan's 'fire and energy and brilliant *sententiae*'. Dr. Johnson (in his *Life of Rowe*) amplified Quintilian: 'Lucan is distinguished by a kind of dictatorial or philosophick dignity, rather, as Quintilian observes, declamatory than poetical; full of ambitious morality and pointed sentences, comprised in vigorous and animated lines.'

Here are the reasons why critics side with Quintilian rather than Martial's bookseller. A poet should teach and delight; one who has 'dictatorial dignity' and 'ambitious morality' soon wearies his readers and forfeits their good will. Secondly, a poem (whether a song or an epic) should be a unity; so many excellent parts do not make an excellent whole. And it is true that the excellence of Lucan lies in his *sententiae*, sometimes in a whole paragraph or speech; seldom (if ever) in a whole episode or book; not at all in the poem as a whole.

These are the most serious shortcomings of Lucan. The others for which he is generally criticized are his monotonous rhythm, his indulgence in the macabre or horrific, his furious partisanship: Petronius also found fault with him for doing without the *deorum ministeria*. All these criticisms can be summed up by saying that Lucan's fault was that he was not Virgil.

Lucan's training, of course, was based on Virgil; but his instinct not to imitate the master so much as to absorb and transform, was correct. The poems of Silius, Statius and Valerius, while they have virtues which Lucan does not have, are less powerful: yet the one imitates the rhythm and diction of Virgil, the others draw their subjects from mythology and build the epic round a hero. They are less demanding than Lucan to read—and less deserving to be read.

For the truth is that Lucan, most successfully of the four later epic poets, attempted to reflect (and yet to mould) the tastes of his time. The age of Nero was aesthetically far more exciting than that of his immediate predecessors and successors. Its symbol is the Golden House rather than the Colosseum; and whatever disregard of the rights of the common people this may imply, it means that among the rich, the educated and the intelligent there was an appreciative circle ready to applaud the creations of new authors. Virgil had been the prophet of the Augustan revolution; Nero and his circle intended to herald a new Augustan age, a cultural revival after the barren years of Tiberius, Gaius and Claudius. But, leaving aside the matter of comparative genius (*could* there have been a second Virgil?), they were doomed to failure for a number of reasons. Firstly, the personality of Nero, unable to accept a rival. Secondly, his auto-cratic policies, leading inevitably to a revival of republicanism among those same people who were, or were intended to be, the leaders of the cultural revolution. Thus there was far less of an appearance of unity, even in the early years; no one from the heart could say *Deus, deus ille, Menalca*; or, like Juvenal in his later years, place all his hopes in the Emperor. Such self-identification with the person of the *princeps* and his cause in any case was an impossibility when the intelligentsia had (comparatively speaking) but shallow roots in the Roman tradition: an unbridgeable gulf separates Virgil and Livy, born under the Republic, from the Annaei, whose loyalties were expected to be primarily to the family of Caesar, not to Rome.

Lucan exemplifies this; the Republicanism of his poem is primarily intellectual, however strongly felt This was inevitable, given the poet's training The rhetoric of the closing years of the Republic was for use as well as for show; the rhetoric in which Lucan was trained had little relation to the arts of persuasion among free men. The poet was constrained to impress as much as to persuade: he could not let his message permeate, as could Virgil. There is, therefore, in rhetorical poetry, no relaxation, no periods when the reader (if he so chooses) may let the poetry gently lap round him, only to surprise him, as Keats says, 'by a fine excess'. This essential quality of poetry is missing in Lucan; there can be no 'fine excess' when everything is already at the highest pitch. This absence of variation in intensity means also that the words themselves are constrained: in the pointed style the *sententia* appeals primarily to the mind, and once it is grasped there is no more to be won from it. In true poetry there should be an infinite opportunity for one reader to find more meanings or less than another in a given passage: this quality of allusiveness or ambiguity is seldom achieved in rhetorical poetry, and the use of symbol and image tends, as a result, to be less subtle than, for example, in the poetry of Virgil.

Yet Lucan's *Bellum Civile* is a poem; it is not a speech (or a series of declamations) nor, by any stretch of the imagination, could it be called history. It is epic, but epic that is changed in its terms. Like Virgil Lucan has a story to relate—the self-destruction of the Roman Republic—and a moral purpose; but the latter predominates and the story proceeds fitfully (the first book is a good example). Where there is so much effort to persuade, the other main function of the poet (to amuse or delight) tends to be relegated to separate episodes, which in another age would be called digressions. Lucan and his contemporaries are censured for their choice of subjects— such as necromancy and herpetology: but this was the taste of the age, and it is a rash critic who attempts to give an objective definition of good and bad taste. What is important is that the conventions of epic poetry in the time of Nero allowed the inclusion of extraneous disquisitions whose connection with the main development of the epic hardly justifies (in our view) their length. These episodes had to be carefully composed; they had to display a knowledge of the literary tradition and a knowledge, often very detailed, of the subject being dealt with. In style they had to be, if possible, dramatic and colourful, vibrant with hyperbole and epigram.

If these, then, are the elements of rhetorical epic, we should accept Quintilian's judgement only with reservations. The foregoing studies have demonstrated Lucan's brilliant rhetorical technique; but if we relate Lucan's poem to the culture of the age of Nero, then we must admit that the poet, as well as the orator, could learn from it (unless we deny the title of 'poetry' to any non-Virgilian epic). Unfortunately, Lucan's very brilliance obscures the more ordinary epic virtues: for he does, in fact, have a story to relate and he does have some concept of characterization, although Caesar, Pompey and Cato are in general too formal to be credible. Above all, he has the sense of drama, of the rise and fall of human fortunes. Had he lived to complete his work he would, I believe, have found it developing more in the direction of tragedy than of traditional epic. And in the final analysis it is this concept, of men and their affairs being driven along by forces greater than themselves, that indubitably places Lucan where he belongs—among the poets.

SELECT BIBLIOGRAPHY

Abbreviations

A.J.P.	*American Journal of Philology.*
C.P.	*Classical Philology*
C.Q.	*Classical Quarterly*
R-E.	Pauly-Wissowa-Kroll, *Real-Encyclopädie d. Klassischen Altertums-wissenschaft*
R.E.L.	*Revue des Études Latines*
Rh.M.	*Rheinisches Museum für Philologie*
T.A.P.A.	*Transactions and Proceedings of the American Philological Association*

The first page-number of each article is given.

Texts, etc.

A. Bourgéry and M. Ponchont (Budé ed., 2 vols.), Paris 1926-9.

J. D. Duff (Loeb text and translation), London 1928.

C. E. Haskins, with Introduction by W. E. Heitland, London 1887.

A. E. Housman, 2nd ed., Oxford 1950 (rev. of 1st ed. by E. Fraenkel, *Gnomon* 2 (1926), 497).

P. Lejay, Book 1, Paris 1894.

R. J. Getty, Book 1, Cambridge 1955

O. A. W. Dilke, Book 7, Cambridge 1960 (revision of J. P. Postgate's ed., Cambridge 1913).

J. P. Postgate, Book 8, Cambridge 1917.

J. Endt, *Adnotationes super Lucanum* (Teubner), Leipzig 1909.

B. M. Marti, *Arnulfi Aurelianensis Glosule super Lucanum*, Rome 1958.

H. Usener, *Commenta Bernensia* (Teubner), Leipzig 1869.

R. J. Deferrari and others, *A Concordance of Lucan*, Washington 1940.

Other works

J. Aymard, *Quelques Séries de Comparaisons chez Lucain*, Montpelier 1951.

J. W. Basore, 'Direct Speech in Lucan as an Element of Epic Technic', *T.A.P.A.* 35 (1904), xciv.

S. F. Bonner, *Roman Declamation*, Liverpool 1949.

H. Bornecque, *Les Déclamations et les Déclamateurs d'après Sénèque le Père*, Lille 1902.

A. Bourgéry, 'Lucain et la Magie', *R.E.L.* 6 (1928), 299.

J. Brisset, *Les Idées Politiques de Lucain*, Paris 1964.

R. T. Bruère, 'Palaepharsalus, Pharsalus, Pharsalia', *C.P.* 46 (1951), 111.

—— 'Lucan's Cornelia', *C.P.* 46 (1951), 221.

M. L. Clarke, *Rhetoric at Rome*, London 1953.

B. Dick, 'The technique of Prophecy in Lucan', *T.A.P.A.* 94 (1963), 37.

L. Eckardt, *Exkurse und Ekphraseis bei Lucan*, Heidelberg 1936.

L. Fahz, *De Poetarum Romanorum Doctrina Magica*, Gieszen 1904.

C. S. Floratos, Ἡ προφήτεια τοῦ P. Nigidius Figulus, Athens 1958.

E. Fraenkel, 'Lucan als Mittler des Antiken Pathos', *Vorträge der Bibliothek Warburg*, 1924, 229.

W-H. Friedrich, 'Episches Unwetter', *Festschr. B. Snell*, Munich 1956, 77.

R. Fritzsche, *Quaestiones Lucaneae*, Jena 1892.

F. Furbringer, *De Somniis in Romanorum Poetarum Carminibus Narratis*, Jena 1912.

R. J. Getty, 'The Astrology of P. Nigidius Figulus', *C.Q.* 35 (1941), 17.

—— 'Neophythagoreanism in Lucan', *T.A.P.A.* 91 (1960), 310.

A. Gregorius, *De M. A. Lucani Pharsaliae Tropis*, Leipzig 1893.

A. Guillemin, 'L'Inspiration Virgilienne dans la Pharsale', *R.E.L.* 29 (1951), 214.

A. Gwynn, *Roman Education from Cicero to Quintilian*, Oxford 1926.

M. Hadas, 'Later Latin Epic and Lucan', *Cl. Weekly* 29 (1936), 157.

H. Haffter, 'Dem schwanken Zünglein lauschend wächte Cäsar dort', *Museum Helveticum* 14 (1957), 118.

R. Helm, 'Lucan', *Lustrum* 1 (1957), 163.

C. Hosius in A. Fleckeisen's *Neuer Jahrb. für Class. Phil.*, 1892, Pt. i, 337.

—— 'Lucan und seine Quellen', *Rh. M.* 48 (1893), 380.

—— *De Imitatione Scriptorum Romanorum imprimis Lucani*, Greifswald 1907.

W. Kroll, 'Das historische Epos', *Sokrates* 4 (1916), 2.

C. Liedloff, *De Tempestatis*, etc., *Descriptionibus*, Leipzig 1884.

H. C. Lipscomb, *Aspects of the Speech in Later Roman Epic*, Baltimore 1909.

E. Malcovati, *Lucano*, Milan 1940.

B. M. Marti, 'The Meaning of the Pharsalia', *A.J.P.* 66 (1945), 352.

F. Marx, art. 'Annaeus' no. 9, *R-E.* i, col. 2226.

A. Oltramare, *Les Origines de la Diatribe Romaine*, Lausanne 1926.

U. Piacentini, *Osservazioni sulla Tecnica Epica di Lucano*, Berlin 1963.

R. Pichon, *Les Sources de Lucain*, Paris 1912.

M. Rambaud, 'L'Apologie de Pompée par Lucain au Livre vii de la Pharsale', *R.E.L.* 33 (1955), 258.

H. J. Rose, 'The Dream of Pompey', *Acta Classica* 1 (1958), 80.

W. Rutz, 'Die Träume des Pompeius in Lucans Pharsalia', *Hermes* 91 (1963), 334.

—— 'Lucan, 1943–1963', *Lustrum* 9 (1964), 243.

E. de St. Denis, *Le Rôle de la Mer dans la Poésie Latine*, Paris 1935.

E. M. Sanford, 'Lucan and his Roman Critics', *C.P.* 26 (1931), 233.

F. Schwemmler, *De Lucano Manilii Imitatore*, Gieszen 1916.

K. Seitz, 'Der Pathetische Erzählstil Lucans', *Hermes* 93 (1965), 204.

F. Streich, *De Exemplis atque Comparationibus apud Senecam, Lucanum*, etc., Breslau 1913.

J. Stroux, 'Die Stoische Beurteilung Alexanders d.G.', *Philologus* 88 (1933), 222.

H. P. Syndikus, *Lucans Gedicht vom Bürgerkrieg*, Munich 1958.

A. Thierfelder, 'Der Dichter Lucan', *Archiv für Kulturgeschichte* 25 (1934), 14.

B. Ullmann, 'History and Tragedy', *T.A.P.A.* 73 (1942), 25.

J. G. Wetzel, *Quomodo Poetae Epici et Graeci et Romani Somnia Descripserint*, Berlin 1931.

A. Hudson-Williams, Note on Lucan 7. 40–44, *C.Q.* (N.S.) 4 (1954), 187.

M. Wünsch, *Lucan-Interpretationen*, Leipzig 1930.

INDEX

LIST OF PRINCIPAL PASSAGES IN LUCAN DISCUSSED